UNITED IRELAND, HUMAN RIGHTS AND INTERNATIONAL LAW

UNITED IRELAND
HUMAN RIGHTS
AND
INTERNATIONAL LAW

FRANCIS A. BOYLE

CLARITY PRESS, INC.

© 2012 Francis A. Boyle
ISBN: 978-0-9833539-2-8
EBOOK ISBN:

In-house editor: Diana G. Collier
Cover: R. Jordan P. Santos

Library of Congress Cataloging-in-Publication Data

Boyle, Francis Anthony, 1950-
   United Ireland, human rights and international law / by Francis A. Boyle.
      p. cm.
   Includes bibliographical references and index.
   ISBN 978-0-9833539-2-8 (alk. paper)
   1. Ireland--International status. 2. Northern Ireland--International status. I.
Title.

KZ4166.B69 2011
341.2'9--dc23

                                 2011036909

Clarity Press, Inc.
Ste. 469, 3277 Roswell Rd. NE
Atlanta, GA. 30305 , USA
http://www.claritypress.com

TABLE OF CONTENTS

Terence Boyle, of Killeacle, Ardfert Kerry, is grandfather to the author.

DEDICATION

TERENCE BOYLE
KILLEACLE, ARDFERT
COUNTY KERRY

Terence Boyle, of Killeacle, Ardfert Kerry, is grandfather to the author. In 1972 Francis A. Boyle, Jr. was able to locate lost Ardfert relatives by asking an old man there, who replied, "Ter Boyle, I knew him well. He was a great poet. The greatest poet in the county. When I was but a wee lad, my father took me to yonder pub and we would listen to the great Ter Boyle recite his poetry. You have relatives here."

To date, just one of Ter Boyle's poems, recorded by the Irish Folklore Commission, has been recovered. In his poem, "Old Billie Crosbie,"[1] the poet confronts the restless ghost of Ardfert's major landowner, William Talbot Crosbie, who inherited lands originally re-assigned (c 1600-1607) as a penal settlement for the purpose of transplanting Irish clans. Between 1841 and 1861, William Crosbie, notoriously known as "Billie the Leveler," saw the Ardfert population reduced by 70%. In the 1870s, when Terence was born, Crosbie carried out "the Ardfert clearance," decried in the *Tralee Chronicle*, (1871) as an effort to "starve and strangle its remaining vitality."

Crosbie wanted to expand his estate by enclosing the village into his domain. To accomplish this, he engaged a process whereby he increased rents to be so impossibly high that few could pay. Things were worse for those who agreed to pay—they became among the most destitute. Crosbie drove people from their homes and shops by force, dispossessing a majority of the hard-working population, leaving few structures standing.[2] Somehow, Ardfert and Ter Boyle survived.

In 1919, the Crosbie family fled Ardfert, soon returning to England. In 1922, their Great House was burned out, paving the way for most of the estate lands to be eventually re-distributed by the Irish Land Commission. With publication of his poem, Terence Boyle gets the last word on the demise of that era.

Ter Boyle lived through difficult years of land wars, the Easter Rebellion, and the Independence War—all hard fought in Kerry. As early as 1914, two thousand "Volunteers" marched in Kerry. At a meeting in Ardfert that same year, "A large proportion of the Volunteers carried rifles and it was an inspiring sight to see in the historic village of Ardfert the steady tramp of armed men who were out for the sole purpose of guarding the future destiny of the Irish nation, " reported *The Kerryman*. The meeting ended with a resolution "that we—the Ardfert Volunteer Corps, hereby beg to congratulate the leader and members of the Irish Party in restoring her freedom to our native land and that we pledge ourselves to maintaining that freedom", followed by the singing of 'A Nation Once Again'.[3]

Terence Boyle's name is included among those credited for their active service during the Independence War in the *Official Roll Book of A (Ardfert) Company of Oglaigh na hEireann (I.R.A.), 2nd Battalion, Kerry No. 1 Brigade I.R.A., 11th July, 1921*, honored by Company Captain John Kearney, Ballyrobert, as follows:

> A (Ardfert) Company, 2nd Battalion I.R.A. comprised 93
> Officers and men. They were the men who took part in
> all the activities of A Company. They were never absent
> from duty. During the Winter of 1920 and the Spring
> and Summer of 1921 they were on active service all
> the time. How often on dark and cold winter nights
> these great men were called on to cut and barricade
> the Company's roads and bridges to hinder enemy
> movements. Scouts had to be on all roads, as the
> Company area was only 2.5 miles from Tralee town
> where a big force of Military, Auxiliaries, and Black
> and Tans were posted. They also had their list of dead
> and wounded. Law and order had to be kept and all
> the hard work of the Company had to be looked after.
> These young men had to do their own home work too.
> The men of A (Ardfert) Company who risked their lives
> will go down in history. As the Officer in Charge I thank
> all these loyal and brave men who helped to get for our
> people the freedom we have today.[4]

Terence Boyle was in his late 40's during that service in 1920 and 1921. Ter's wife, Brigid (Murphy) Boyle hailed from nearby Causeway, Kerry, where the battles were almost as bad. The war was fought everywhere—on the streets, in the fields, on all roads, in shops, in farmhouses, in the barns. For eight of the nine months preceding that hard-won 1921 ceasefire, Brigid Boyle was pregnant with son Francis Anthony Boyle I.

The Boyle family continues to research reports on the circumstances of Ter's hasty 1921 emigration with his wife and children. No one doubts that his crops failed that year. Francis Boyle Sr. told his sons that, at that time, Ter's brother was being held far offshore on a prison ship—in order to make escape or rescue more difficult. "Murph— Herself" as Brigid was known, simply informed her grandchildren, "You are all old Sinn Feiners." Terence and Brigid both spoke the Irish language.

by Virginia Anne Clare Boyle, II, Bard of the Boyle Family
September 6, 2011
Gabh mo leithscéal, (lit.: Please accept my half-story).

Endnotes

1   Source: O'Connor, Tommy. *Ardfert in Times Past: A History of Ardfert Parish, County Kerry from Earliest Times.* Farranwilliam, Ardfert: 1999, p. 197.
2   *Id*, p. 164-169.
3   *Id*, p.209.
4   *Id*, p. 217.

The Boyle family continues to research reports on the circumstances of Ter's hasty 1927 emigration with his wife and children. No one doubts that his crocodile tear that year. Francis Boyle Sr. told his sons that at that time, Tor's brother was being held far offshore on a prison ship — in order to make escape or rescue more difficult. "Maggie — Herself," as Brigid was known, simply informed her grandchildren, "You are all old Sinn Feiners." Terence and Brigid both spoke the Irish language.

by Virginia Anne Clare Boyle, II, Bard of the Boyle Family
September 6, 2011
Gabh mo leithscéal, dit.. Please accept my half-story.

Endnotes

1. Spencer O'Connor, Tommy. Antrim in Times Past: A History of Ardten, etc. Ballymena: Bann Publishers. Times I, etc. williams. Antrim, 1996, p. 192.
2. Ibid., p. 151-169.
3. Id. p. 206.
4. Ibid., p. 211.

Proclamation of the Irish Republic
issued 24 April 1916
Poblacht na h-Éireann
The Provisional Government
of the Irish Republic
to the People of Ireland

Irishmen and Irishwomen: In the name of God and of the dead generations from which she receives her old tradition of nationhood, Ireland, through us, summons her children to her flag and strikes for her freedom.

Having organised and trained her manhood through her secret revolutionary organisation, the Irish Republican Brotherhood, and through her open military organisations, the Irish Volunteers and the Irish Citizen Army, having patiently perfected her discipline, having resolutely waited for the right moment to reveal itself, she now seizes that moment, and, supported by her exiled children in America and by gallant allies in Europe, but relying in the first on her own strength, she strikes in full confidence of victory.

We declare the right of the people of Ireland to the ownership of Ireland, and to the unfettered control of Irish destinies, to be sovereign and indefeasible. The long usurpation of that right by a foreign people and government has not extinguished the right, nor can it ever be extinguished except by the destruction of the Irish people. In every generation the Irish people have asserted their right to national freedom and sovereignty; six times during the past three hundred years they have asserted it in arms. Standing on that fundamental right and again asserting it in arms in the face of the world, we hereby proclaim the Irish

Republic as a sovereign independent state, and we pledge our lives and the lives of our comrades-in-arms to the cause of its freedom, of its welfare, and of its exaltation among the nations.

The Irish Republic is entitled to, and hereby claims, the allegiance of every Irishman and Irishwoman. The Republic guarantees religious and civil liberty, equal rights and equal opportunities to all its citizens, and declares its resolve to pursue the happiness and prosperity of the whole nation and of all its parts, cherishing all the children of the nation equally, and oblivious to the differences carefully fostered by an alien government, which have divided a minority from the majority in the past.

Until our arms have brought the opportune moment for the establishment of a permanent national government, representative of the whole people of Ireland, and elected by the suffrages of all her men and women, the Provisional Government, hereby constituted, will administer the civil and military affairs of the Republic in trust for the people. We place the cause of the Irish Republic under the protection of the Most High God, whose blessing we invoke upon our arms, and we pray that no one who serves the cause will dishonour it by cowardice, inhumanity, or rapine. In this supreme hour the Irish Nation must, by its valour and discipline, and by the readiness of its children to sacrifice themselves for the common good, prove itself worthy of the august destiny to which it is called.

Signed on behalf of the provisional government,

Thomas J. Clarke, Sean MacDiarmada, Thomas MacDonagh, P. H. Pearse, Eamonn Ceannt, James Connolly, Joseph Plunkett

INTRODUCTION

What follows in this book are the efforts by one Irish American dual-national to further promote the complete and final realization of this 1916 Proclamation of the Irish Republic throughout the entire Island of Ireland and for all of the Irish People living there without distinction by means of international law, human rights law, and U.S. Constitutional law during the past three decades. Others will have their own stories to tell. But this is mine.

The Irish Republic was created by this Proclamation as an independent state on Easter Monday 1916. Pursuant thereto, the 1916 Proclamation was followed up by General Elections held in December of 1918 resulting in the establishment of the First Irish National Parliament. The Dail Eireann enacted a Declaration of Independence on January 21, 1919 that "in the name of the Irish Nation, ratify the establishment of the Irish Republic and pledge ourselves and our people to make this declaration effective by every means at our command." The 1916 Irish Republic still exists today as a legal entity under international law and practice.[1]

As of now, however, the 1916 Irish Republic has been illegally partitioned by Britain between the state known as the Republic of Ireland that governs 26 counties of the Irish Republic and the British colonial enclave known as "Northern Ireland" that illegally occupies the six Northeast counties of the Irish Republic. For want of a more convenient moniker, I will refer to this illegal British colonial enclave as "Northern Ireland" for the rest of this book. As such Northern Ireland is subject to the well-established rules of international law requiring the decolonization of colonial enclaves that are analyzed below in chapter 2.[2]

Notice here as well that the state known today as the Republic of Ireland is a constituent unit of the Irish Republic that was proclaimed in 1916 and was never lawfully terminated. Ex iniuria ius non oritur—law does not arise from injustice—is a foundational principle of public international law and of human rights law: Law does not arise from injustice! Britain's partition of the 1916 Irish Republic was and still is null and void ab initio under peremptory norms of international law, including and especially the right of the Irish People to self-determination.

How the Republic of Ireland and Northern Ireland can be merged into a United Ireland in order to finalize the 1916 Proclamation of the Irish Republic will be discussed below in the final chapter to this book.

This illegal colonial partition of the 1916 Irish Republic by Britain has created enormous political, military, legal, human rights, and economic problems for all the Irish People living on both sides of this completely arbitrary, capricious, and evanescent partition line. I speak here from firsthand experience. In 1986 I took a car tour of the so-called partition line. Repeatedly my Irish companions and I could not determine where Northern Ireland began and where the Republic of Ireland left off. That was because each entity is a component unit of the 1916 Irish Republic whose partition was artificially contrived and illegally imposed by Britain.

To be sure, during the past three decades I have not dealt with most of the legal and human rights problems produced by Britain's colonial military occupation of the six Northeast counties of the 1916 Irish Republic. But I have attempted to grapple with and resolve many of the most critical issues that have presented themselves internationally, especially here in the United States. All of these efforts have been motivated and guided by the vision of United Ireland as articulated in the 1916 Proclamation of the Irish Republic and that was faithfully conveyed to me by my father, who was conceived in Ireland. His uncle had fought against Britain in the Irish War for Independence, and was ultimately incarcerated by Britain on a prison ship because he was deemed to be an incorrigible revolutionary. That we are, in the Boyle Family. And proud of it!

In this regard, starting in June of 1987 the author served as legal advisor to the Palestine Liberation Organization (P.L.O.) on the drafting of the November 15, 1988 Palestinian Declaration of Independence and the creation of the State of Palestine.[3] During the course of our deliberations we considered two sources as models for the Palestinian Declaration of Independence: the American Declaration of Independence of July 4, 1776; and, at my advice, the 1916 Proclamation of the Irish Republic. At their request, I still remember proudly and personally faxing to the P.L.O. a copy of the 1916 Irish Proclamation of Independence. I also incorporated numerous other legal and historical lessons learned from Ireland's revolutionary War for Independence against Britain into the advice that I gave the P.L.O.

For example, I advised the P.L.O. that because Palestine was going to be proclaimed "In the Name of God, the Compassionate, the Merciful," they must proclaim the Palestinian State from their capital in Jerusalem and there in front of the Al Aqsa Mosque after the close of prayers in the evening. I told the P.L.O. that this act of defiance of and independence from the illegal, colonial Israeli military occupation regime would replicate the 1916 Proclamation of the Irish Republic by Pádraig Pearse, acting in the name of the Provisional Government of the Irish Republic, standing outside the General Post Office in downtown Dublin, surrounded by British troops. That Pearse and his fellow co-signors of the 1916 Proclamation were all later murdered by Britain, but that the Irish Free State emerged in 1922 as a result of their heroism and sacrifice. As the Irish National Poet William Butler Yeats aptly put it in his classic poem *Easter, 1916*: "...A terrible beauty is born...."

I told the P.L.O. that since I was not a Palestinian, it would be inappropriate for me to perform this sacred task, but that it had to be done by someone even at the risk of his life. So it was done! My Irish American heart and soul were with that brave and courageous Palestinian who read their Declaration of Independence in front of Al Aqsa Mosque in the evening at the close of prayers on November 15, 1988, now known as Palestine Independence Day. Today the P.L.O. Executive Committee serves as the Provisional Government for the State of Palestine that has Observer State status with the United Nations Organization and is bilaterally recognized de jure by about 127 other states. I view it as Irish America's contribution to Palestine and the Palestinians.

The Irish and the Palestinian anti-colonial struggles for complete and final independence from the most brutal, longstanding, illegal, military occupation regimes perpetrated against them by Britain and Israel continue apace today. But history records that it was Britain that was ultimately responsible for illegally partitioning both Ireland and Palestine in gross violation of the right to self-determination of the Irish and the Palestinians. Indeed, at almost the exact same time as it was partitioning Palestine, Britain likewise carved-up its Raj over the Indian subcontinent into the two states of India and Pakistan, deliberately igniting yet another human rights catastrophe for hundreds of thousands of completely innocent human beings as it was then contemporaneously inflicting upon the Palestinians. Divida et impera— just as the Roman Empire had done before Britain.

More recently, from 1992 to 1995, Britain actively promoted and eventually obtained the criminal carve-up of the Republic of Bosnia and Herzegovina—a U.N. member state—with the same anti-humanitarian effects (see chapter 1) upon countless numbers of innocent human beings in Bosnia.[4] Plus ça change, plus ça reste la meme chose.

This receptivity to the Irish experience of revolution and

independence by the P.L.O. should come as no surprise. Whenever I travel around the world people are well aware of the fact that it was the Irish who fought the first successful anti-colonial war of national liberation in the twentieth century, and against the mightiest empire in world history as of that time: "Great" Britain. For the past ten decades Ireland and the Irish have been beacons of liberty, freedom, hope, inspiration, and defiance against overwhelming power and incredible odds to the oppressed and downtrodden peoples and nations all over the world.

A future United Ireland along the lines of and fulfilling the promise of the 1916 Proclamation of the Irish Republic is an inevitability. The only remaining questions are when and how. But in Ireland time has always been the enemy of peace. Let us work and hope toward achieving United Ireland peacefully and in accordance with and by means of implementing international law and human rights for all Irish living on the Island of Ireland without discrimination.

Toward that end, this book has been written.

Endnotes

1   *See* Sean MacBride, S.C., *Introduction* to IRELAND'S RIGHT TO SOVEREIGNTY, INDEPENDENCE AND UNITY IS INALIENABLE AND INDEFEASIBLE (n.d.) (copy on file with author). *See also* Sean MacBride, That Day's Struggle: A Memoir 1904-1951 (Caitriona Lawlor ed. 2005).

2   Felix Ermacora, *Colonies and Colonial Regime,* 1 Encyclopedia of Public International Law 662-66 (1992); Gerhard Hoffmann, *Enclaves,* 2 *Id.* at 80-82 (1995); Josef Brink, *Non-Self-Governing-Territories,* 10 *Id.* at 316-21 (1987).

3   See Francis A. Boyle, Palestine, Palestinians, and International Law (2003): *Id.*, Breaking All the Rules: Palestine, Iraq, Iran and the Case for Impeachment (2008); *Id.*, The Palestinian Right of Return under International Law (2011).

4   *See* Francis A. Boyle, The Bosnian People Charge Genocide (1996); Brendan Simms, Unfinest Hour: Britain and the Destruction of Bosnia (2001).

CHAPTER ONE

THE IRISH HECATOMB

THE LEGAL CASE FOR THE POTATO FAMINE AS BRITISH GENOCIDE

'How could they save the Hecatomb sacrificed at Bantry? ...If they raise their voice against oppression they run the risk of being accused of exciting to murder.'
Fr. James Maher
to a Dublin paper, 4 Dec. 1847

In April of 1996 I received a phone call from Mr. James Mullin, Chairman of the Irish Famine Curriculum Committee. He had a problem. They had submitted a copy of their Irish Famine Curriculum to the State of New Jersey Holocaust Education Commission that had a mandate to "recommend curricular material on a wide range of genocides." He had been informed by the Commission that they needed an Expert Opinion on whether the so-called "Irish Potato Famine" qualified as an instance of "genocide." In principle I agreed to provide that Opinion Letter to the Commission, but I first wanted to review their Irish Famine Curriculum for myself. It was entitled *The Great Irish Famine*.

Upon examination of their Irish Famine Curriculum, I concluded as a professional educator since 1976 when I first taught in the College of Harvard University, that this was an excellent set of instructional materials that should be made available to high school students. Therefore, I drafted an Opinion Letter to the New Jersey Holocaust Commission expressing my expert opinion that the so-called "Irish Potato Famine" was really a case of British genocide against the Irish. Here is what I had to say:

May 2, 1996

Dr. Paul B. Winkler
Executive Director
and
Steven E. Some
Chairperson
New Jersey Commission on Holocaust Education
CN 500
Trenton, New Jersey 08625

Dear Friends:

As I understand it, your Commission was created by the New Jersey Legislature in 1991 to prepare curriculum materials on the Holocaust for use in the state's public schools. In 1994, your mandate was expanded "to study and recommend curricular material on a wide range of genocides." Because I am a Professor of International Law with experience arguing on matters of genocide before the International Court of Justice in The Hague (the so-called World Court of the United Nations System), I have been asked by the Chairman of the Irish Famine Curriculum Committee to give you my opinion on the question whether the policies pursued by the British government from 1845 to 1850 in Ireland that resulted in the mass starvation of over one million Irish People constituted "genocide." My answer is in the affirmative for the reasons explained below. This opinion is based in part on the facts set forth in The *Great Irish Famine* that has already been submitted to you by the Irish Famine Curriculum Committee.

The United States government is a party to the 1948 Convention on the Prevention and Punishment of the Crime of Genocide. This Genocide Convention is a Treaty of the United States and therefore "...the Supreme Law of the Land..." according to Article VI of the United States Constitution, the so-called Supremacy Clause. Hence, as a State Agency, your Commission is bound to follow the terms of the Genocide Convention whenever relevant to your activities. I respectfully submit that your Commission is obliged to pay attention to the definition of "genocide" set forth in the Genocide Convention when interpreting your 1994 statutory mandate "to study and recommend curricular material on a wide range of genocides."

"Genocide" is a legal term with a precise definition that has been determined by the 1948 Genocide Convention. Article II of the Genocide Convention provides as follows:

Article II

In the present Convention, genocide means *any of the following acts* committed with intent to destroy, in whole or in part, a national, ethnical, racial or religious group, as such:

(a) Killing members of the group;
(b) Causing serious bodily or mental harm to members of the group;
(c) Deliberately inflicting on the group conditions of life calculated to bring about its physical destruction in whole or in part;
(d) Imposing measures intended to prevent births within the group;
(e) Forcibly transferring children of the group to another group. [Emphasis added.]

Clearly, during the years 1845 to 1850, the British government pursued a policy of mass starvation in Ireland with intent to destroy in substantial part the national, ethnical, and racial group commonly known as the Irish People, as such. In addition, this British policy of mass starvation in Ireland clearly caused serious bodily and mental harm to members of the Irish People within the meaning of Genocide Convention Article II(b).

Furthermore, this British policy of mass starvation in Ireland deliberately inflicted on the Irish People conditions of life calculated to bring about their physical destruction in substantial part within the meaning of Article II(c) of the 1948 Genocide Convention. Therefore, during the years 1845 to 1850 the British government knowingly pursued a policy of mass starvation in Ireland that constituted acts of genocide against the Irish People within the meaning of Article II(b) and Article II(c) of the 1948 Genocide Convention.

Pursuant to Article V of the Genocide Convention, the Congress of the United States of America adopted what is called implementing legislation for the Genocide Convention that makes genocide a crime under U.S. Federal Criminal Law. Basically following the terms of the Genocide Convention, this Genocide Convention Implementation Act of 1987 (found in Title 18 of the United States Code) defines the crime of "genocide" as follows:

§1901. Genocide

(a) BASIC OFFENSE.—Whoever, whether in time of peace or in time of war, in a circumstance described in subsection (d) and with the specific intent to destroy, in whole or in substantial part, a national, ethnic, racial, or religious group as such—

(1) kills members of that group:
(2) *causes serious bodily injury to members of that group;*
(3) causes the permanent impairment of the mental faculties of members of the group through drugs, torture, or similar techniques;
(4) *subjects the group to conditions of life that are intended to cause the physical destruction of the group in whole or in part;*
(5) imposes measures intended to prevent births within the group; or
(6) transfers by force children of the group to another group;

or attempts to do so, shall be punished as provided in subsection (b). [Emphasis added.]

Clearly, the policy of mass starvation pursued by the British government in Ireland from 1845 to 1850 caused "serious bodily injury to members of" the Irish People and therefore constituted "genocide" as defined by 18 U.S.C. §1901(a)(2). In addition, this British policy of mass starvation pursued in Ireland from 1845 to 1850 also subjected the Irish People "to conditions of life that [were] intended to cause the physical destruction of the group in whole or in part" and thus constituted "genocide" as defined by 18 U.S.C. § 1901(a)(4). Hence, this 1845-1850 British policy of mass starvation against the Irish People would qualify as "genocide" within the meaning of both §1901(a)(2) and § 1901(a)(4) of Title 18 of the United States Code.

Therefore, in accordance with the legal definition of genocide found in the 1948 Genocide Convention and the 1987 Genocide Convention Implementation Act, the British policy of mass starvation pursued in Ireland from 1845 to 1850 constituted "genocide" against the Irish People. Furthermore, in my opinion as an educator and as a practicing international lawyer who has successfully argued the matter of genocide before the

International Court of Justice, the British policy of genocide by means of mass starvation pursued against the Irish People from 1845 to 1850 should certainly be included within the curriculum of any course dealing with the perpetration of "genocides" in the modern world: e.g., against the Jewish People, against the Armenians, against Native Americans, against African Americans under slavery, etc.

All of these contemporary historical examples would clearly constitute "genocide" within the definitional provisions of the 1948 Genocide Convention and the 1987 Genocide Convention Implementation Act, and thus fall within your 1994 statutory mandate "to study and recommend curricular material on a wide range of genocides."

If I can be of any further assistance to you in this matter, please feel free to contact me directly as indicated above.

Yours very truly,

Francis A. Boyle
Professor of International Law

cc: James Mullin, Chairman
Irish Famine Curriculum Committee

My Opinion Letter together with another letter provided by Professor Charles Rice of Notre Dame Law School did the trick. The Irish Famine Curriculum was approved for use in New Jersey's schools on September 10, 1996. Then in October of 1996 New York Governor George Pataki signed an education law mandating instruction on this British campaign of inflicting mass starvation in Ireland as genocide in New York public schools. But by then all hell had broken loose.

The British government and its academic fellow-travelers and punditorial sycophants proceeded to launch a massive attack in the U.S. news media against the Irish Famine Curriculum. The basic thrust of their disingenuous critique was that the so-called "Potato Famine" was not of similar scope as the Nazi Holocaust against the Jews and therefore it did not qualify as "genocide." Of course the Nazi Holocaust against six million Jews was historically and numerically not the same thing as Britain's deliberate starvation of over one million Irish. Yet both cases of mass atrocities inflicted by the Nazis and the British, respectively, each qualified as "genocide" for the reasons explained above.

In order to refute this claim definitively, my brother Jerome and I drafted a *Statement* entitled **The Famine Was Genocide.** We then transmitted it to Mr. Owen Rodgers, Chairman of the Irish Famine Genocide Committee. He then proceeded to line up endorsements of our *Statement* by approximately 125 distinguished personalities, most of whom were lawyers or professional educators, and many of whom were not even Irish. Mr. Rodgers and his Committee then had our *Statement* published as an advertisement in *The Irish Echo* for February 26 – March 4, 1997, together with all of the endorsements by name and title. For limitations of space, I will only reprint our *Statement* here without the personal endorsements:

The Famine Was Genocide

Irish Echo/February 26-March 4, 1997

Some controversy has surrounded the use of the word "genocide" with regard to the Great Irish Famine of 150 years ago. But this controversy has its source in an apparent misunderstanding of the meaning of genocide. No, the British government did not inflict on the Irish the abject horrors of the Nazi Holocaust. But the definition of "genocide" reaches beyond such ghastly behavior to encompass other reprehensible acts designed to destroy a people.

As demonstrated by the following *legal* analysis, the Famine was genocide within the meaning of *both* United States and *International law.*

The United States Government is party to the 1948 Convention On The Prevention And Punishment of the Crime of Genocide ("Genocide Convention"). As a Treaty of the United States, the Genocide Convention is therefore "the Supreme Law of the land" under Article VI of the U.S. Constitution. The U.S. Government has also passed implementing legislation which substantially adopts the Genocide Convention and makes any violation of the Convention punishable under federal law. 18 U.S.C. § 1901.

Article II of the Genocide Convention provides:

In the present Convention, genocide means *any of the following acts* committed with intent to destroy, in whole or in part, a national, ethnical, racial or religious group as such:

(a) Killing members of the group;

(b) *Causing serious bodily or mental harm to members of the group;*

(c) *Deliberately inflicting on the group conditions of life calculated to bring about its physical destruction in whole or in part;*

(d) Imposing measures intended to prevent births within a group;

(e) Forcibly transferring children of the group to another group.

(Emphasis supplied)

From 1845-50, the British government pursued a policy of mass starvation in Ireland with the intent to destroy in substantial part the national, ethnical and racial group known as the Irish People. This British policy caused serious bodily and mental harm to the Irish People within the meaning of Genocide Convention Article II(b). This British policy also deliberately inflicted on the Irish People conditions of life calculated to bring about their physical destruction within the meaning of Article II(c) of the Convention. Therefore, from 1845-50 the British government knowingly pursued a policy of mass starvation in Ireland which constituted acts of Genocide against the Irish People within the meaning of Article II(b) and (c) of the 1948 Genocide Convention.

While there are many legitimate subjects of debate surrounding the Famine, there is no doubt that the British Government committed genocide against the Irish People. This particular "debate" should therefore come to an end.[1]

For what it is worth, it is my most respectful advice to all Irish not to use the words "Holocaust" or "Shoah" to refer to the British mass starvation campaign against the Irish. Out of respect for the suffering of the Jewish people, I believe we Irish should permit them to monopolize those two terms and not in any way, shape, or form use them or try to appropriate them for ourselves unless we are specifically referring to the Nazi Holocaust or Shoah against the Jews. It is for this reason that

I have respectfully suggested in this chapter that as an alternative we Irish consider using the term "Hecatomb": The British Hecatomb against the Irish.

Certainly like other groups subjected to genocide we Irish are entitled to employ one word to sum up and encapsulate the unique experience of Britain deliberately and systematically starving to death one million Irish over a period of five years. I nominate Hecatomb. But whatever you want to call it, this Irish Hecatomb clearly constituted "genocide" for the reasons explained and endorsed above by our 125 colleagues.

Previously, I had encountered and refuted this completely disingenuous, deceptive and bogus argument against labeling a genocide as what it truly is, when I was the lawyer for the Republic of Bosnia and Herzegovina arguing their genocide case against Yugoslavia before the International Court of Justice, which is otherwise known as the World Court.[2] There the genocidal Yugoslavia was represented by Shabtai Rosenne from Israel as their lawyer against me. Rosenne proceeded to argue to the World Court that since he was an Israeli Jew, what Yugoslavia had done to the Bosnians was not the equivalent of the Nazi Holocaust against the Jews and therefore did not qualify as "genocide" within the meaning of the 1948 Genocide Convention.

I rebutted Rosenne by arguing to the World Court that you did not need an equivalent to the Nazi Holocaust against the Jews in order to find that an atrocity constituted "genocide" in violation of the 1948 Genocide Convention. Indeed the entire purpose of the 1948 Genocide Convention was to prevent another Nazi Holocaust against the Jews. That is why Article I of the Genocide Convention clearly provided: "The Contracting Parties confirm that genocide, whether committed in time of peace or in time of war, is a crime under international law which they undertake *to prevent* and to punish." (Emphasis supplied.) You did not need six million dead human beings in order to constitute "genocide." The one million Irish that Britain deliberately starved to death was certainly sufficient.

Furthermore, in support of my 1993 genocide argument to the World Court for Bosnia, I submitted that Article II of the 1948 Genocide Convention expressly provided: "In the present Convention, genocide means any of the following acts committed with the intent to destroy, *in whole or in part*, a national, ethnical, racial or religious group, as such..." (Emphasis supplied.) In other words, that to be guilty of genocide a government did not have to intend to destroy the "whole" group as the Nazis intended to do with the Jews. Rather, a government can be guilty of genocide if it intends to destroy a mere "part" of the group.

Francis A. Boyle (far left), on the floor of the World Court in 1993, squaring off against his adversary Shabtai Rosenne (far right) of Israel representing the genocidal Yugoslavia, just before he argued and then won the first of his two World Court Orders overwhelmingly in favor of Bosnia and Herzegovina on the basis of the 1948 Genocide Convention.

Certainly Yugoslavia did intend to exterminate all Bosnian Muslims if they could have gotten away with it, as manifested by their subsequent mass extermination of at least 7,000 Bosnian Muslim men and boys at Srebrenica in July of 1995.

But in 1993 it was not necessary for me to argue to the World Court that Yugoslavia intended to exterminate *all* the Bosnian Muslims. Rather I argued to the World Court that at that point in time the best estimate was that Yugoslavia had exterminated about 200,000 Bosnians out of the population of about 4 million Bosnians, including therein about 2.5 million Bosnian Muslims. Therefore, I argued to the World Court that these dead victims constituted a "substantial part" of the group and that the appropriate interpretation of the words "or in part" set forth in Article II of the Genocide Convention should mean a "substantial part."

The World Court emphatically agreed with me and rejected Rosenne's specious, reprehensible, and deplorable arguments. So on 8 April 1993 the International Court of Justice issued an Order for three provisional measures of protection on behalf of the Republic of Bosnia and Herzegovina against Yugoslavia that were overwhelmingly in favor of Bosnia as follows:

52. For these reasons,
    The COURT,

Indicates, pending its final decision in the proceedings instituted on 20 March 1993 by the Republic of Bosnia and Herzegovina against the Federal Republic of Yugoslavia (Serbia and Montenegro), the following provisional measures:

A. (1) Unanimously,

The Government of the Federal Republic of Yugoslavia (Serbia and Montenegro) should immediately, in pursuance of its undertaking in the Convention on the Prevention and Punishment of the Crime of Genocide of 9 December 1948, take all measures within its power to prevent commission of the crime of genocide;

(2) By 13 votes to 1,

The Government of the Federal Republic of Yugoslavia (Serbia and Montenegro) should in particular ensure that any military, paramilitary or irregular armed units which may be directed or supported by it, as well as any organizations and persons which may be subject to its control, direction or influence, do not commit any acts of genocide, of conspiracy to commit genocide, of direct and public incitement to commit genocide, or of complicity in genocide, whether directed against the Muslim population of Bosnia and Herzegovina or against any other national, ethnical, racial or religious group;

IN FAVOUR: *President* Sir Robert Jennings; *Vice-President* Oda; *Judges* Ago, Schwebel, Bedjaoui, Ni, Evensen, Guillaume, Shahabuddeen, Aguilar Mawdsley, Weeramantry, Ranjeva, Ajibola;

AGAINST: *Judge Tarassov* [from Russia];

B. Unanimously,

The Government of the Federal Republic of Yugoslavia (Serbia and Montenegro) and the Government of the Republic of Bosnia and Herzegovina should not take any action and should ensure that no action is taken which may aggravate or extend the existing dispute over the prevention or punishment of the crime of genocide, or render it more difficult of solution.

This World Court Order for the indication of provisional measures of protection was the international equivalent of a U.S. domestic Temporary Restraining Order and Injunction combined.

The Order was binding international law. Under the terms of United Nations Charter Article 94(2), the World Court submitted this Order to the U.N. Security Council for enforcement—just like any Judge would submit its Order to a Sheriff for enforcement. For political reasons the Security Council failed and refused to enforce this World Court Order prohibiting genocide against Yugoslavia on behalf of the Republic of Bosnia and Herzegovina, a U.N. member state.[3]

Consequently, I decided to return to the World Court for a second Order. I knew full well that no government had ever won two such Orders in one case in the entire history of the World Court going back to when it was founded in 1921. But I had no alternative: Yugoslavia was exterminating the Bosnians right before my very eyes. I could watch the Bosnian genocide live on CNN.

Once again Rosenne argued against me. This time he was assisted by three Serbian lawyers, whom I dismissively referred to as Moe, Larry, and Curly—the Three Stooges. I won that Second Order for an additional three provisional measures of protection for the Republic of Bosnia and Herzegovina against the genocidal Yugoslavia that was overwhelmingly in favor of Bosnia from the World Court on 13 September 1993 by 13 votes to 2, 13 votes to 2, and 14 votes to 1, respectively. This was the first time ever in the history of the World Court going back to 1921 that any government had ever won two such Orders in one case. I had won six different provisional measures of protection from genocide on behalf of the Republic of Bosnia and Herzegovina against Yugoslavia in under six months.

Pursuant to my advice and with the authorization of President Izetbegovic, on 10 November 1993 I was instructed by the Bosnian Ambassador to the United Nations (later Foreign Minister) Muhamed Sacribey to institute legal proceedings against Britain for violating the Genocide Convention and the Racial Discrimination Convention. On 15 November 1993 Ambassador Sacribey convened a press conference at U.N. Headquarters in New York in which he stated Bosnia's solemn intention to institute legal proceedings against the United Kingdom for genocide. Later that day, I filed with the World Court a *Communication* that I had drafted, which was entitled *Statement of Intention by the Republic of Bosnia and Herzegovina to Institute Legal Proceedings Against the United Kingdom Before the International Court of Justice.* Ambassador Sacribey had also distributed this *Statement* at his press conference in New York. [4]

Since Ambassador Sacirbey was not a professional international lawyer, immediately after his press conference to announce our genocide lawsuit before the World Court against Britain held at U.N. Headquarters in New York City, he referred all the world's news media to me in order to answer any questions they might have. Soon thereafter I was contacted by the British news media conglomerate Reuters News Agency asking for an extensive interview on this entire matter that would be used as a background information source to be provided to the rest of the British news media in order to prepare their own stories on it. I readily agreed to give this extensive interview to Reuters.

During the course of this interview with Reuters I spent a good deal of time explaining the historical origins of the 1948 Genocide Convention originating out of the Nazi Holocaust against the Jews. When I was finished giving this brief historical disquisition, the Reuters reporter asked me: "Professor Boyle, are you Jewish?" I immediately responded: "No, I'm Irish. But my People know all about genocide!"

My comment was front page news headlines all over Britain the next day. The most lurid headline came from the tabloid *Daily Mail* in bold and capital letters on the front page: **IRISH LAWYER JOINS FIGHT AS MUSLIMS CRY "MURDER."** [5] That headline warmed the inner recesses of my Irish heart and soul and brought a big smile to my face: "When Irish eyes are smiling..." Their story continued with me saying: "It's always the case where there has been an underdog in the world, you have always found people of Irish descent with the underdog. After having suffered so much, Irish people can immediately empathise with people who suffer all over the world."

On 30 November 1993, by telephone I personally informed Ambassador Sacirbey in Geneva that these documents were ready to be filed with the World Court at any time. But by then it was too late. In immediate reaction to our public *Statement* of Bosnia's intention to institute legal proceedings against the United Kingdom on 15 November 1993 for genocide, a Spokesman for the British Foreign Office said that this announcement "would make it difficult to sustain the morale and commitment of those [British troops and aid workers] in Bosnia in dangerous circumstances." The report continued: "Foreign Office sources said there were no plans to remove the Coldstream Guards, who have just begun a six-month deployment to Bosnia. But Whitehall would take account of whether the Bosnian threat of legal action was in fact taken to the International Court of Justice in The Hague."[6] At that time all humanitarian relief supplies for the Bosnians including food was flown in by military transports from Ramstein airbase in Germany to Sarajevo airport, which was then under the control of British and French troops. I had no doubt that in the harsh winter of 1993 Britain would have starved to death 2.5 million Bosnians just as it had previously starved to death 1 million Irish. For these reasons of severe duress and threats perpetrated by Britain and other European states, the Republic of Bosnia and Herzegovina was forced to withdraw from those World Court proceedings for genocide against the United Kingdom by means of concluding with it a coerced "Joint Statement" of 20 December 1993.

Before Britain threatened Bosnia with mass starvation during the harsh winter of 1993, I was then in negotiations with the World Court for their convening an Emergency Hearing on my Request for provisional measures of protection against Britain for aiding and abetting genocide against Bosnia that was to take place sometime before Christmas Day 1993. In other words, I had effectively "won" the argument: The World Court was going to hear me out on my claims against Britain for aiding and abetting genocide against Bosnia.

I am certain that I would have won something for Bosnia against Britain from the World Court on the basis of the 1948 Genocide Convention. That is precisely why Britain threatened to starve the Bosnians to death during the harsh winter of 1993. Be that as it may, I am the only lawyer in the entire world with experience at having tried to sue Britain on the basis the 1948 Genocide Convention before the International Court of Justice.

In its final Judgment on the merits in the *Bosnia* case that was issued in 2007, the World Court definitively agreed with me once and for all time that in order to constitute genocide, a state must only intend to destroy a "substantial part" of the group "as such":

198. In terms of that question of law, the Court refers to three matters relevant to the determination of "part" of the "group" for the purposes of Article II. In the first place, the intent must be to destroy at least a substantial part of the particular group. That is demanded by the very nature of the crime of genocide: since the object and purpose of the Convention as a whole is to prevent the intentional destruction of groups, the part targeted must be significant enough to have an impact on the group as a whole. That requirement of substantiality is supported by consistent rulings of the ICTY and the International Criminal Tribunal for Rwanda (ICTR) and by the Commentary of the ILC to its Articles in the draft Code of Crimes against the Peace and Security of mankind (e.g. *Krstić*, IT-98-33-A, Appeals Chamber Judgment, 19 April 2004, paras. 8-11 and the cases of *Kayishema, Byilishema,* and *Semanza* there referred to; and *Yearbook of the International Law Commission,* 1996, Vol. II, Part Two, p. 45, para. 8 of the Commentary to Article 17).[7]

In other words, in order to find Britain guilty of genocide against the Irish, it is not required to prove that Britain had the intention to exterminate *all* Irish. Rather, all that is necessary is to establish that Britain intended to destroy a "substantial part" of the Irish People. A million people out of a population of about eight million Irish whom Britain deliberately and systematically starved to death certainly constitutes a "substantial part" of the Irish People.

Furthermore, in paragraphs 293 and 294 of its 26 February 2007 *Bosnian* Judgment, the World Court found that you did not even need a million exterminated people in order to constitute genocide, let alone six million. Rather, even the seven thousand murdered Bosnian Muslim men and boys at Srebrenica were enough to constitute genocide. These victims constituted about one-fifth of the Srebrenica community.

Proving that the so-called "Famine" was really British genocide against the Irish would require a separate book of its own that perhaps someday I will have the pleasure, the time, and the resources to write. In the meantime, however, concerning the factual—not legal—basis for the claim that the so-called "Famine" constituted British genocide against the Irish, I refer the reader to two excellent and comparatively recent volumes of scholarly research conducted by Dr. Christine Kinealy: **This Great Calamity** (1995) and **A Death-Dealing Famine** (1997). To this list of leading evidentiary factual sources for proving genocide, I would also add the pathbreaking work of scholarship by Cecil Woodham-Smith, **The Great Hunger** (1962). To be sure, these and other works of historical research and scholarship do not express an authoritative opinion on the legal issue of "genocide" because their authors were historians, not international lawyers.

But briefly in this regard, concerning the criminal intent by Britain to destroy the Irish "as such" and in "substantial part" that is required to prove the charge of "genocide," Britain together with its academic sycophants and punditorial fellow-travelers have argued that the so-called "Famine" was produced by rigid adherence to *laissez-faire* economics by the British government at the time. In accordance with the 1948 Genocide Convention, extermination must be with "intent to destroy, in whole or in part, a national, ethnical, racial or religious group, as such." Hence, the basic thrust of the argument by these pro-British apologists is that this supposed "economic" motivation somehow exculpates Britain from any charge of genocide against the Irish arising out of the "Famine." Even taking this specious argument at face value—which I do not—it is analogous to the Nazi Doctrine of "useless eaters" which targeted people with disabilities for extermination, and was soundly condemned by the Nuremberg Tribunal in its 1946 *Judgment* convicting most of the top Nazi leaders for their mass atrocities committed during World War II. In fact, these pro-British apologists are all Irish Hecatomb Deniers!

Irrespective of Britain's alleged and self-exculpatory *laissez-faire* economic "motivation," there is more than enough historical evidence to prove that the British government specifically intended to destroy the Irish "as such" and in "substantial part" as required to establish genocide under the 1948 Genocide Convention. Anglo-American criminal law has always made a fundamental distinction between "motive" (the reason *why* an act is committed) and "intent" (the conscious *will to commit* an act). It affixes criminal responsibility to the "intent" of the actor; and this principle of law holds true irrespective of the "motive" of the actor. Despite pro-British legalistic pettifoggery, there is more than enough evidence from the British historical archives that at the time of the so-called "Famine" the highest level officials in the British government specifically *intended* to destroy the Irish "as such" and in "substantial part" by means of their starvation policies irrespective of their alleged motivation of profiting from the exercise of so-called *laissez-faire* economics.

Below, I will briefly summarize only some of the historical evidence manifesting genocidal intent against the Irish by the concerned

British government officials that is based upon research conducted by reputable scholars derived from Britain's own historical archives and sources. In particular I would like especially to draw to the reader's attention official documents and statements referred to below that were produced and made by British government officials acting within their scope of official duties that constitute direct evidence of their genocidal intent against the Irish.

These official documents and statements bind Britain as a matter of international law today. I could take these official British government documents and statements to the International Court of Justice in The Hague and use them to prove Britain's specific intent to destroy the Irish "as such" and in "substantial part" in order to prove genocide as I twice succeeded in doing with official documents produced by Yugoslavia and statements uttered by Slobodan Milosevic and his henchmen during the lawsuit for genocide that I filed at the World Court for the Republic of Bosnia and Herzegovina against Yugoslavia. These official documents and statements constitute what we lawyers call Admissions Against Interest, and self-incriminate Britain for committing genocide against the Irish.

There are many other historical sources that prove that Britain did indeed specifically intend to destroy a "substantial part" of the Irish people "as such" by means of its mass starvation campaign in Ireland that it waged from about 1845 to about 1852. If and when I should be fortunate enough to have the opportunity to file a lawsuit for genocide against Britain before the International Court of Justice on behalf of the Irish People, I will be certain to compile them all—just as I twice successfully did for the Republic of Bosnia and Herzegovina against Yugoslavia. And I will win this genocide argument too—this time for the Irish!

Evidence of Genocidal Intent by Britain
Against the Irish During the So-called "Famine"

Cast of British Genocidaires Against the Irish

Charles Trevelyan
> Architect of the genocide, Assistant Secretary of the Treasury in charge of poor relief in Ireland

John Russell
> Prime Minister

Charles Wood
> Chancellor of the Exchequer, strong supporter of Trevelyan's

policies, claimed the British treasury could not afford to assist Ireland

Henry John Temple (Palmerston)
> Irish Peer, Foreign Secretary, he pushed Russell to adopt harsher measures and personally profited from them

William Gregory
> Author of the "Gregory Clause" which limited poor aid law to those who owned less than ¼ acre of land, the crucial element which forced small landowners to sell or abandon their claims in the face of starvation.

George Grey
> Home Secretary

Alfred Power
> Twistleton's replacement after he resigned, Trevelyan henchman

Randolph Routh
> Chief Member of the relief commission

John Fox Burgoyne
> Irish Famine Commissioner, Major-General

Nassau Senior
> Economic theorist whose writings encouraged the British to let the Irish die off.

George William Frederick Villiers (Clarendon)
> Viceroy of Ireland

Edward Twistleton
> Poor law commissioner who eventually resigned in protest against the British policy of extermination.

From Christine Kinealy, This Great Calamity (1995) (footnotes omitted) (emphasis added).

Page 16. ...Malthus, however, offered a solution. The population of Ireland...had to be reduced. ...
Page 17. ... In regard to the breeding habits of the Irish poor,

[Malthus] explained that they were so degraded that they were apt to 'propagate their species like brutes' and therefore should not be considered as human. ...

Page 51. ... At the beginning of July 1846, the Treasury decided that the supplies in the various good depots *should be allowed to run out and not be replenished.* ...

Page 72. ... In early September [1846], the Irish Executive warned the government that intervention in the affairs of Ireland was imperative 'to save the people from starvation'. ... In the short term, the government's commitment to non-intervention might appear cruel but, as *The Times* pointed out, *'There are times when something like harshness is the greatest humanity'.*

Page 74-75. ...Russell had no intention of allowing his government to repeat the experiment and stated unequivocally: 'It must be thoroughly understood that we cannot feed the people. It was a cruel delusion to pretend to do so.'

Page 78. ...As had already been agreed [by Trevelyan], grain would not be sent to Ireland or any depots opened until the government believed it to be absolutely necessary. *Moreover, Scotland was to be supplied with imported food before any could be sent to Ireland.*

Page 79. ...The final two months of 1846...amidst growing reports of death from starvation ...the verdict given at some inquests was 'Wilful murder against Lord John Russell'. ...

...Even in Skibbereen, Co. Cork, ...1846 ...[with] daily reports of deaths from starvation, no exception was to be made. ... Trevelyan explained to Routh. "You must be prepared to act with great firmness and to incur much obloquy..."

Page 87. ...By the end of 1846, there were increasing reports that the population was living on seaweed...

Page 96. Impervious to such reports, the official philosophy of the Board of Works continued to be 'to keep the numbers as low as the existing calamity will permit.'

Page 97. ... In the west of Ireland, an increasing number of verdicts of death from starvation were blamed upon the inadequacy of the relief works. Jones admitted that the condition of these people meant that relief in return for labour was starving the people who 'their bodily strength gone and spirits depressed, they have not the power to exert themselves sufficiently to earn the ordinary day's wages'.

Page 102. ...The increase in deaths from starvation became so commonplace that many newspapers stopped reporting them in detail...The policy of dismissing large numbers from the relief works regardless of whether or not an alternative form of relief was available was widely criticized within Ireland. The Kerry Grand Jury described the decision to strike 20 per cent of labourers off the relief lists as a 'death warrant'.

Page 103. ...[O'Brien, MP Co. Limerick] estimated that 240,000 persons had died of starvation unnecessarily, as the government possessed the means of preventing this.

Page 111. ...The government refused to provide any financial support to the Poor Law...

Page 118. ... [Labouchere, the Chief Secretary] informed Russell:

> The workhouses are full and the people are turned away to perish. ... The mortality in the workhouse is rapidly increasing, ...

Page 119. In January 1847. ...the government was receiving over 100 reports each day of deaths from starvation, and they believed this to be an under-estimation.

Page 134. ... The extended Poor Law, therefore, was regarded not merely as an agent for the provision of relief, but also as a catalyst for facilitating important economic and social improvements in Ireland. This was felt to be particularly necessary in the south and west of Ireland because:

> The owners and holders of land in these districts had permitted or encouraged the growth of the *excessive population* which depended upon the precarious potato and they alone had it in their power to restore society to a safe and healthy state.

Page 136. ...the government...acknowledged that: "...instances of starvation daily occur."

Page 169. At the end of March 1847, Lord George Bentinck, leader of the Tory opposition, questioned the government regarding the number of deaths in Ireland and accused the Whigs of attempting to conceal the truth...:

> They know the people have been dying by their thousands and I dare them to enquire what has been the number of those who have died through their mismanagement, by their principles of free trade. *Yes, free trade in the lives of the Irish people.*

Page 183. ... Again, the character of the people was cited both as a justification for a stringent application of relief and for the need for social change.

Page 186. ... Twistleton... anticipated a continuation of deaths from starvation for which, he believed, he would be held responsible.

Page 195. ... If this was not possible, the guardians were to discharge the old and infirm paupers who were already in the workhouse to make way for able-bodied applicants for relief.

Page 196. ...The Rathkeale guardians...unanimously decided to resign in protest against the policy of making the most vulnerable categories of paupers leave the shelter of the workhouses...

Page 200. ... For a people who were already debilitated by three consecutive years of shortages, however, the physical exertion of stone-breaking undoubtedly proved exhausting and possibly the last straw for those already weakened by hunger and a diet lacking in nutrition.

Page 213. ...As Twistleton pointed out to Trevelyan....

> It is wished that the Irish should not come upon the national finances for the relief of their destitute. It is also wished that deaths from starvation should not take place. But these wishes are as unreasonable as if you ask us to make beer without malt, or to fly without wings.

Page 221. ...Some leading members of the government, however, were concerned that if, as a consequence of a literal interpretation of the [Gregory] Clause, there was an increase in deaths from starvation, they might be held to blame.

Page 224. One of the most common causes of suffering arising from the Gregory Clause was the fact that the families of a person occupying more than a quarter acre of land were denied relief. This punitive regulation was thought to contribute to an increase in the number of deserted wives and abandoned children...

Page 227. ... Twistleton...believed that if the government continued to insist that local rates must support local poverty, they were running a risk of increased deaths from starvation. ...

Page 228. ... Trevelyan explained that *the policy of the government had been purposely designed* to make the people choose between:

> ... a lamentable loss of life of the lower classes, and the temporary distress of those classes whose duty it is to give employment to able bodied poor and gratuitous relief for the impotent poor.

Page 230. ...Twistleton predicted that there was a risk of further deaths from starvation. ...

Page 231. ... Underpinning this was a strong conviction that God's purpose, with the help of the political economists, was to be served by forcing the inadequacies of the poorest parts of Ireland to be met from within their own resources... The ultimate recipients of the relief remained victims to a system of parsimony that viewed their very existence as part of the problem.

Page 235. In the Kilrush union, in the six-month period from July to December 1848, 6,090 people were evicted from their holdings. ...

Page 236. ... The local Inspector described these evictions as 'inhuman' acts which had been perpetrated on a 'helpless, hopeless people'.

Page 239. ...the Poor Law Commissioners...described the blight as having reduced the condition of the people in the west of Ireland 'to nearly the lowest point of squalor and want at which human beings can exist'. ...Twistleton warned:

Unless funds from some extraneous sources are placed at their disposal for the aid of the Distressed Unions it cannot be doubted that deaths from starvation will occur in some of these unions as in the winter of 1846-7.

Page 240. ... Twistleton was afraid that if the precise details about the quantity of relief provided were made public, *'others might say that we are slowly murdering the peasantry by the scantiness of the relief'*...

Page 245. ... Once more, the distressed people were held as hostages to a dogmatic government policy, as interpreted by its most powerful agent, the Treasury. Balancing the imperial ledgers appeared to be more important than saving lives...

Page 246. ...Trevelyan suggested to the Poor Law Commissioners that all children should be put out of the workhouses to make additional room for able-bodied men. ...

Page 249. ... God, [Trevelyan] believed, had ordained the Famine to teach the Irish people a lesson, and the machinations of man should not seek to reduce the effects of such a lesson...

Page 250. ... Because of the refusal of the Treasury to heed their advice, the Commissioners informed the Treasury that they considered themselves to be:

absolved from any responsibility on account of deaths which may take place in consequence of those privations.

Page 250. ...The Census Commissioners acting on behalf of

the government, stated that in 1849 mortality reached a new peak. ...

Page 251. ...However, Cormac Ó Grádas *estimate of approximately one million excess deaths...appears to be the most accurate calculation to date.*

Page 258. ...if the Act of Union was a true union between kingdoms, then all parts of the United Kingdom shared an equal responsibility for helping to relieve the distress in another part. The Rate-in-Aid, however, placed the burden of relieving Irish distress very firmly on Ireland itself. ...

Part 263. ...Twistleton... emphasized the fact that *the various policies introduced by the British government were not due to a shortage of funds but to an unwillingness to continue providing support to Irish distress...*

Page 267. ... The 1849 Amendment Act also facilitated the emigration of Irish paupers to the British colonies, paid for out of the poor rates. ...

Page 272. ...In the Scariff union in Co. Clare, the local Poor Law Inspector blamed the recent increase in deaths from starvation on the irregularity in the supply of food to paupers in receipt of outdoor relief. ...

Page 286. ...The Commissioners were particularly anxious that young females in the workhouse—of which there was a disproportionately large number—should be trained in all domestic duties in order to make them suitable candidates for emigration. ...

Pages 295-296. ... In the 1850s, the Census Commissioners recorded that in the ten years from 1841 to 1851 the population of Ireland had fallen from 8,175,124 persons to 6,552,385 persons. They also estimated that if the Famine had not occurred, the population of Ireland in 1851 would have been 9,018,799. ... *Regardless of the high social and economic cost, the Census Commissioners suggested Ireland had benefited from the Famine.* ... This example of *post hoc* rationalisation comes close to suggesting that mass starvation, death, eviction, and large scale emigration were legitimate tools of social engineering.

Page 305. ... At the same time, emigration would relieve Ireland of her *excess population* and provide British colonies with much needed settlers.

Page 311. To a large extent, the administrators of the Poor Law were anxious to promote pauper emigration as far as possible. ... One Inspector suggested to the boards of guardians in his district that if this class of paupers were sent to Canada:

Some of the permanent dead weight in the workhouse may be got rid of at a cost to the electoral division of about five pounds...

Page 315. ... Wood, the Chancellor of the Exchequer, agreed that a vigorous collection of the rates was necessary to encourage even more emigration. ... The Prime Minister ... summed up the situation thus: 'it is better that some should sink, than that they should drag others down to sink with them'. ...

Page 316. ...The orphan emigration scheme was carried out at no cost to the government, the major part of the expenditure being met by the colonial authorities themselves. ...

Page 318. The scheme to assist orphaned workhouse inmates to emigrate was welcomed by the Poor Law Commissioners. ... It was also a way of relieving the impoverished western workhouse of some of their *excess population* at relatively little cost. ...

Page 319. The majority of boards of guardians regarded the orphan emigration scheme favourably as it provided a way of emptying their workhouses of a class of paupers who were, potentially, a long-term burden on the proof rates. ...

Page 326. ... Many boards of guardians were anxious that, if possible, the workhouses should be cleared of female orphans, and many applied to the Emigration Commissioners for financial aid for this purpose.

Page 334. ... The government, however, continued to be reluctant to intervene or do anything which might impede the flow of migrants from Ireland, something which they believed would ultimately be beneficial to Ireland and which, furthermore, was taking place at no cost to the state.

Page 336. The English, Welsh and Scottish Poor Law authorities responded to the unprecedented influx of Irish poor with large-scale removal, some of which was not only indiscriminate but also illegal. Furthermore, many of the removed paupers were abandoned at the nearest port in Ireland rather than being taken to their place of origin. ...

Page 339. ... The guardians of the North Dublin union demanded that the Irish Poor Law Commissioners prosecute the English Poor Law Board for negligence. Regardless of the iniquities and abuses of the Laws of Settlement, however, they were not charged.

Page 339. ...The Belfast guardians also disapproved of the way in which the removed paupers were treated, particularly the fact that they were not supplied with food for the journey.

Although the Belfast guardians, like their southern counterparts, frequently petitioned both the Poor Law Commissioners and the British government for a change in the Law, no change was made. Page 340. ... The inability of an Irish pauper to acquire the same entitlements as a British pauper reinforced the unequal status of Irish paupers in Britain and highlighted the difficulties which faced all Irish immigrants, no matter how long their residence in Britain.

Page 343. ... The government responded to this potentially more serious situation [1846 blight] by *reducing its involvement in the import of food into the country and by making relief more difficult to obtain.*

Page 348. ... It was perhaps ironic that as the demand for relief increased markedly in 1846, Russell's government was determined that its involvement should decrease. ...

Page 351. ...the amount provided by the British Treasury was derisory. It has been estimated as only 0.3 per cent of the annual gross national product of the United Kingdom. ...

Page 352. ...By implementing a policy which insisted that local resources must be exhausted before an external agency would intervene, and pursuing this policy vigorously despite local advice to the contrary, the government made suffering an unavoidable consequence of the various relief systems which it introduced. The suffering was exacerbated by the frequent delays in the provision of relief even after it had been granted and by the small quantity of relief provided, which was also of low nutritional value. ... *Nor could the government pretend ignorance of the nature and extent of human tragedy* that unfolded in Ireland following the appearance of blight. The Irish Executive and the Poor Law Commissioners sent regular, detailed reports of conditions within the localities and increasingly requested that even more extensive relief be provided. In addition, Trevelyan employed his own independent sources of information on local conditions, by-passing the existing official sources of the Lord Lieutenant. This information revealed the extent of deprivation caused by the Famine. ...

Page 353. ... As the Famine progressed, it became apparent that the government was using its information not merely to help it formulate its relief policies but also as an opportunity to facilitate various long-desired changes within Ireland. These included *population control* and the consolidation of property through a variety of means, including emigration, the elimination of small holdings, and the sale of large but bankrupt estates. This was a pervasive and powerful 'hidden agenda'. The government measured the success of its relief policies by the changes which were brought about in Ireland rather than by the quality of relief provided *per se*. The public declaration of the Census Commissioners in the Report of the 1851 Census, which stated that Ireland had benefited from the changes brought about by the Famine, is a clear example of this. ... Despite the overwhelming evidence of prolonged distress caused by successive years of potato blight, the underlying philosophy of the relief efforts was that they should be kept to a minimalist level; in fact they actually decreased as the Famine progressed. The reduction in the relief provided both in real terms and in nutritional value inevitably had a detrimental, and frequently fatal, impact upon the health of the distressed population. ...

Page 354. ...The policy of closing ports during periods of shortages in order to keep home-grown food for domestic consumption had on earlier occasions proved to be an effective way of staving off famine within Ireland. ... By refusing to allow a similar policy to be adopted in 1846-7, despite the recommendations of the Lord Lieutenant, the British government ensured that 'Black 47' was indelibly associated with suffering, famine, mortality, emigration and to some, misrule.

Page 357. ... The government was able to use the chaos caused by the Famine to facilitate a number of social and economic changes. In particular, ... Irish peasants, feckless and indolent as they were perceived to be, were judged less 'worthy' to receive relief than their counterparts in Britain. One consequence of this perception occurred in 1846 when Ireland was not allowed to receive imports of food until supplies had been delivered to Scotland first. ...

From Christine Kinealy, A Death-Dealing Famine (1997) (footnotes omitted) (emphasis added).

Page 2. ... Between 1846 and 1851, at least one million people died out of a base population of over eight million people. To this can be added the high mortality amongst emigrants, which may have accounted for a further 100,000 deaths. Furthermore, many of the survivors of the Famine years experienced shortened lifespan as a consequence of successive years of privation. ...

Page 4. ... At the end of 1847, Trevelyan declared the Famine to be over, despite the fact that 1.5 million people were still dependent on a minimal and punitive form of state assistance. ... the Famine, which he described as 'the judgment of God on an indolent and unself-reliant people,' a people, moreover, who liked to 'make a poor mouth'...

Page 9. After 1846, the decision by the government not to close the ports to export of food allowed Irish merchants to seek markets where prices were highest; this inevitably meant those outside of Ireland. This led to Mitchel's claim that more food was continuing to leave Ireland than was coming into the country.

Page 29. ... In the early nineteenth century, Ireland not only fed her own population, but was a net exporter of food. ...

Page 51. ... This sentiment was given official endorsement by Sir Randolph Routh, the Chief Commissioner in charge of relief operations during 1845-46. In his opinion [to Trevelyan]: The little industry called for to rear the potato, and its prolific growth, leave the people to indolence and all kinds of vice, which habitual labour and a higher order of food would prevent, *I think it very probable that we may derive much advantage from this present calamity.*

Page 71. ... This was clearly stated by Clarendon in 1847. When discussing the condition of the Irish, he posed the rhetorical question, 'We shall be equally blamed for keeping them alive or letting them die ...' Two years later, Russell, lamenting that he was unable to do more for the starving Irish, stated: "...let us not grant, clothe etc. etc. any more and see what they will do."

Page 77. The most controversial aspect of Whig policy was its decision not to continue Peel's programme of importing Indian corn, but to leave food supply to market forces . ... *they decided not to close the ports to keep food within Ireland* nor to forbid distillation of grain to take place. These measures were all traditional responses to food shortages and the refusal by the Whig government to implement them marked a radical departure of official policy from earlier subsistence crises. ...

Page 79. ...The high level of exports demonstrated that food production was still high even as people starved in Ireland. ...

Page 82. ... The Lord Lieutenant, Bessborough, warned Russell that there was a growing belief that the government should have done more to make food accessible to the destitute...:

"...but it is difficult to persuade a starving population that one class should be permitted to make 50 per cent profit by the sale of provisions whilst they are dying in want of these."

Page 83. ... Lord Clarendon, who succeeded Bessborough as

Lord Lieutenant, warned Russell that... 'no-one could now venture to dispute the fact that Ireland had been sacrificed to the London corn-dealers because you were a member for the City, and that no distress would have occurred if the exportation of Irish grain had been prohibited'...

Page 84. ... This resulted in an increase in potato exports from Ireland to mainland Europe. ...

Page 98. ... Consequently, the rate of mortality had risen dramatically and, by the beginning of 1847, the Whig government was admitting that 'instances of starvation occur daily'.

Page 103. ... The Relief Commissioners recommended that the amount of food to be provided was to be 'miserable and scanty'. ...

Page 104. ...[I]n the summer of 1847, not all the money voted by the government was spent. The Irish Executive asked if the residue of this money (approximately £500,000) could be reallocated to medical relief, which they considered to be underfunded. The Treasury refused on the grounds that to do so would only further the 'unhealthy dependence' of the Irish people on central government.

Page 105. Although the Temporary Relief Act had stipulated that the soup kitchens could remain open until 30 September 1847, *the government decided to begin closing them in August. ...*

Page 108. ... As the Famine progressed, a number of ideological conflicts emerged between Strzelecki and Trevelyan, especially over the issue of providing relief to children in the west—a scheme which the British Relief Association had successfully pioneered but which Trevelyan regarded as too generous. ...

Page 118. In 1848, starvation and disease were still destroying whole communities in Ireland. A widespread policy of evictions completed the destruction of the potato economies in parts of the south and west. Emigration became an important strategy for survival for those who had the energy or resources to leave the country. ...

Page 122. The Chancellor of the Exchequer [Wood to Clarendon] justified the parsimony of the relief after 1847 on the grounds that, *'except through a purgatory of misery and starvation, I cannot see how Ireland is to emerge into anything approaching either quiet or prosperity'.*

Page 123. ... When it was suggested to William Gregory that the provision would destroy the class of small farmers in Ireland, he replied that 'he did not see of what use such small farmers could possibly be'. ...

Page 125. ... Between 1849 and 1854, approximately 250,000 persons were evicted from their homes, officially and permanently. If illegal evictions and voluntary surrender of land are added, the figure is much greater. ...

Page 126. ... When the Poor Law Commissioner complained of the hardship resulting from these clearances, Trevelyan responded by stating that *only by continuing this process would they 'at last arrive at something like a satisfactory settlement of the country'.* ... A large number of the landed elite and their agents viewed the social dislocation as an opportunity to clear their estates without fear of resistance. ... *Other proprietors, ... cleared [their] estates with the intention of replacing his Catholic tenants with Protestants, preferably from Scotland.*

The way in which evictions were carried out was often ruthless and added to the pain of displacement and homelessness. ...

Page 127. ... In a warning to the Home Secretary, he [Claredon] maintained, 'The case is too shocking for publication if it can be avoided.'... Whilst the politicians were shocked by what they were told, no legislative changes were made. ...

Page 130. ...the Chief Poof Law Commissioner, Edward Twistleton. ... feared that if precise details regarding the scantiness of relief were known in England, public opinion 'might say that *we are slowly murdering the peasantry by the scantiness of the relief'.* ...

Page 136. In 1848 over 50 per cent of the total potato crop was lost. In the west, the crop was almost totally destroyed. ... Twistleton tartly pointed out that the high level of mortality in many unions was painful evidence of the parsimony of the relief provision. ...

Page 137. ... Strzelecki had estimated that the cost of feeding each child was only one-third of a penny each day. Russell personally promised that the scheme would continue even after Count Strzelecki had left Ireland. The promise was not kept and relief provision was further centralized in the already overburdened Poor Law.

Pages 137-38. In private, Trevelyan admitted that the situation in the western unions was critical. *He accepted that unless there was more government intervention, 'the deaths would shock the world and be an eternal blot on the nation and the government will be blamed'.* ...

Page 138. Early in December 1848, Clarendon had warned the government of the possibility of wholesale starvation, which, he cautioned, 'would not only be shocking but bring deep disgrace on the government'. By the end of the month, when his demands for additional aid had failed to elicit any response, … . …Clarendon felt that the greater fault lay with Charles Wood, Charles Trevelyan and George Grey. …

…Clarendon confided to Russell that the situation 'is enough to drive one mad' and asked the prime minister:

>…I don't think there is another legislature in Europe
>that would disregard such suffering as now exists
>in the west of Ireland, *or coldly persist in a policy of*
>*extermination.*

Page 145. … The Treasury's failure to heed Twistleton's repeated pleas for emergency funding led him to declare that he considered he and his colleagues were 'absolved from any responsibility on account of deaths which may take place in consequence of those privations'.

Twistleton opposed the Rate-in-Aid on the grounds that it was the duty of the state and the national Treasury to provide for the areas still suffering from the Famine. …

>… I wish to leave distinctly on record that, from want
>of sufficient food, many persons in these Unions are
>at present dying or wasting away; and, at the same
>time, it is quite possible for this country to prevent the
>occurrence there of any death from starvation , by the
>advance of a few hundred pounds.

…Clarendon… explained to Russell that Twistleton's action had been motivated by the fact that: 'He thinks that the destitution here is so horrible, and the indifference of the House of Commons to it so manifest, that *he is an unfit agent of a policy that must be one of extermination.*

Page 146. … During the Famine, emigration and mortality cleared the poorest counties of a large proportion of their populations at no expense to the government. … *The fact that a large proportion of the emigrants were Catholic was a source of concern to the Church hierarchy. Many members of the government by contrast viewed this fact as desirable,* especially if they could be replaced with Protestant settlers from Britain. Even Clarendon, who had been increasingly sympathetic to the victims of the famine, viewed the disappearance of so many Catholics as a hopeful sign for the future of Ireland. He stated that, 'The departure of thousands of papists Celts must be a blessing to the country they quit' and he was particularly pleased to note that

'Some English and Scottish settlers have arrived.'

Page 148. ... the government was generally pleased that so many poor Catholic peasants left Ireland. In parts of the west, whole communities emigrated. When Twistleton brought this to the attention of Trevelyan, the latter, in an official reply, informed him:

> I do not know how farms are to be consolidated if small farmers do not emigrate, ...we shall at last arrive at something like a satisfactory settlement of the country.

Page 149-150. ... Approximately £10 million was provided by the British government during the Famine period. This represented ½ per cent of Britain's GNP. Most of this money was issued as a loan, which had to be repaid even as the Famine continued. ...

...Archbishop MacHale ...drew an unfavourable comparison with the state's generosity only a decade earlier to slave-owners, who were given £22 million compensation for the abolition of slavery. ...

Page 151. ...*Within a few years, over two million people had disappeared: one million had died, and another one million had emigrated.* The population continued to fall throughout the remainder of the century, a combination of emigration, delayed marriages and celibacy. By 1900, it had fallen to approximately half of its pre-Famine level. The population decline did not finally reverse until the 1960s. ...

...Those who had died as a result of disease, starvation or exhaustion were mostly from the west of the country. Complete famines and whole communities who had subsisted on potatoes prior to 1845 were wiped out. The fact that many of them had been Irish-speaking weakened the use of the Irish language. *By 1851, the number of Irish-speakers had halved.* ...

Page 152. Many of the people who were lost during the Famine were Catholic, except in parts of east Ulster. ...

From Christine Kinealy, *"The Famine Killed Everything" : Living with the Memory of the Great Hunger,* in Ireland's Great Hunger 1-40 (David A. Valone & Christine Kinealy eds. : 2002).

Page 20. ... Trevelyan wrote in 1846, on the eve of the period of greatest suffering, that the blight had been sent to remedy Ireland's social ills, stating:

> the cure has been applied by the direct stroke of an all wise Providence in a manner as unexpected and

unthought of as it is likely to be effectual. God grant
that we may rightly perform our part and not turn into
a curse what was intended for a blessing.

(Trevelyan to Monteagle, 9 October 1846, Monteagle Papers,
NLI)

Page 30. ... By the beginning of 1849 Clarendon had become
totally disillusioned with the policies of his colleagues in London
attesting that:

C. Wood, backed by Grey, and relying on arguments (or
rather, Trevelyanisms) that are no more applicable to
Ireland than to Loo Choo, affirmed that the right thing
to do was to do nothing—they have prevailed and you
see what a fix we are in. (Clarendon to Duke of Bedford,
Letter Books, Bodleian Library, 16 February 1849)

From William B. Rogers, *The Great Hunger: Act of God or Acts of Man?*, in Ireland's Great Hunger 235-56 (David A. Valone & Christine Kinealy eds. : 2002).

Page 250. ... In support of the concept of the Famine as genocide:

• The British had put into place a system of laws over time
that deprived the Irish of much of their land, language, trade,
education, role in government and free practice of religion.

• Longstanding British racism against the Irish people
dehumanized, debased and helped pauperize the Irish, making
the failure to somehow relieve their suffering acceptable to the
British public and government.

• The right of landlords to evict Irish families during the
Famine regardless of circumstances was upheld by the British
government.

• Significant quantities of food were exported from Ireland
during the Famine, justified under the doctrine of laissez-faire and
with the active support of the British government.

• Much of Irish culture was lost, including a significant
majority of all Irish speakers.

• The British could have done more to alleviate the suffering
of the Irish, as demonstrated by Kinealy, Ó Gráda, and others.
(New Jersey Great Irish Famine Curriculum; Genocide Section)

Page 251. In 1849 Edward Twistleton, an Englishman and
the Irish Poor Law Commissioner, resigned to protest lack of aid
from Britain. The Earl of Clarendon, Lord Lieutenant of Ireland,
told British Prime Minister Lord John Russell the same day, " He

(Twistleton) thinks that the destitution here [in Ireland] is so horrible, and the indifference of the House of Commons is so manifest, that he is an unfit agent for a policy that must be one of extermination." In regard to his anger at the lack of support provided to the Famine by the House of Commons, the Earl of Clarendon made his feelings known to Prime Minister Russell. "I do not think there is another legislature in Europe that would disregard such suffering as now exists in the west of Ireland, or coldly persist in a policy of extermination" (Woodham-Smith 380-381). However, politicians like the Earl of Clarendon were in the minority. More crucially, these efforts by leaders, religious groups, and common citizens were obviously not nearly sufficient to stop the suffering and dying.

From Cecil Woodham-Smith, The Great Hunger (1962)(footnotes omitted) (emphasis added).

Page 59. At the time of the famine, Trevelyan ... disapproved of the Irish; ...

Page 63. ... It was easy to issue an order in London that no relief was to be given to what was termed 'ordinary distress'.

Page 67. ...To Routh this was yet another proof of Irish inadequacy: ... 'It is annoying that all these harbours are so insignificant. It shows Providence never intended Ireland to be a great nation.'

Page 70. ... in the Commons, William Smith O'Brien...fiercely attacked the Government. Famine was menacing Ireland, and the Government sent not food but soldiers—Ireland was to starve, and be coerced. ...

Page 71. Throughout these months, as famine, in Routh's words, was 'steadily and gradually approaching', evictions were reported weekly. ... landlords were eager to clear their property of non-paying tenants.

Page 75. Yet through these months and throughout the famine years the 'native produce' of Ireland was leaving her shores in a 'torrent of food.' ... huge quantities of food were exported from Ireland to England throughout the period when the people of Ireland were dying of starvation. ...At first sight the inhumanity of exporting food from a country stricken by famine seems impossible to justify or condone. ...

Page 84. Trevelyan's intentions were very different. Irish relief was to be restricted to a single operation; the government Indian corn, purchased at the order of Sir Robert Peel, was to be placed in depots by the Commissariat, sold to the people–and that was the end. *There was to be no replenishment, even if there was a sum of money in hand from sales; once supplies had been disposed of relief was over.*

Page 85. ...By the end of June, 1846, government supplies were all but exhausted; ...

Page 87. ...Winding up relief was now pushed on vigorously, and on July 8 *Trevelyan rejected a shipload of Indian corn.*

Page 105. ...*Punch*, for instance, published cartoons week after week depicting the Irishman as a filthy, brutal creature, an assassin and a murderer, begging for money, under a pretence of buying food, to spend on weapons. ...

Page 106. Second, the Government would not import or supply any food. There were to be no Government depots to sell meal at a low cost or, in urgent cases, to make free issues, as had been done during last season's failure. No orders were to be sent abroad, nor would any purchases be made by Government in local markets. ...

Page 109. Therefore, the first object of the new plans was to 'check the exorbitant demands of last season'; they were, in fact, designed not to save Ireland but to protect England. ...

Page 110. Outside Government circles, closing the food depots at the moment of total failure appeared inexplicable. ...*Catholic Archbishop John MacHale, ...told Lord John Russell, 'You might as well issue an edict of general starvation as stop the supplies...'* ... No free issues whatever were to be made. ...

Page 111. ...The Chancellor of the Exchequer now ordered that all undertakings must be shut down on August 8, irrespective of whether or not they were completed and of the distress in the district. ...

Page 117. The British Government was not prepared to supply food but very ready to call out troops. ...

Page 142. Lord Monteagle now made a personal appeal to Routh, begging him, in view of the sufferings of the people, to open the depots. Routh refused.

Page 156. These complications confirmed Trevelyan in his low opinion of the Irish. 'The great evil with which we have to contend,' he wrote to Colonel Jones, on December 2, is 'not the physical evil of the famine, but the moral evil of the selfish, perverse and turbulent character of the people.'...

Page 177. ... The thought that famine was the will of God was a consolation to him [Trevelyan], and he hoped that the Catholic priests were making this clear. 'It is hard upon the poor people that they should be deprived of knowing that they are suffering from an affliction of God's providence,' he wrote. ...

Page 227. ... Lord Monteagle, in particular, believed that in emigration lay the solution of Ireland's population problem,... he was also responsible for setting up the Select Committee of the House of Lords on Colonization, that is, emigration, in 1847.

Page 286. ...Certain landlords made use of the seed shortage to get rid of their ruined tenantry; they were, Sir John Burgoyne told Trevelyan, withholding seed from poor tenants...

Page 303. Trevelyan considered the stoppage of rations to have been accomplished smoothly, successfully and painlessly. Three million persons had been on the Government's hands and had been disposed of without an outbreak of violence. ...

Page 310. ...it is still hardly possible to explain, or to condone, the British Governments' determination to throw the Irish destitute on the local Poor rate.

Page 313. ... Sailors' clothing rejected by the Admiralty was suggested, but Routh considered it 'much too good for the Irish poor'. ...

Page 317. ...but on October 23 Lord Clarendon made an urgent appeal to Lord John Russell: ... 'Ireland *cannot be left to her own resources*, they are manifestly insufficient, we are not to let the people die of starvation, we must not believe that rebellion is impossible.' Lord John replied, coldly, 'The state of Ireland for the next few months must be one of great suffering. Unhappily the agitation for Repeal has contrived to destroy nearly all sympathy in this country.'

Page 363. ...and Lord Clarendon told Prince Albert that he looked forward to the winter 'with perfect dismay'; he was afraid that 'a great part of the population must die of absolute want'. The failure of the potato crop in 1848 was as complete as in 1846. ...

Page 366. ...As John Russell warned Clarendon, 'The course of English benevolence is frozen by insult, calumny and rebellion', ...Clarendon pressed for food supplies and relief plans, Lord John Russell told him, 'Neither assistance from public works nor a general system of rations are to be looked to for any large portion of relief, repeating, in a second letter, that it was 'impossible for the Government to do much to relieve distress'. ...

Page 367. Twistleton told Trevelyan that a number of unions would soon be asking for loans, and in a crushing reply Trevelyan told him there would be no loans. ...Though the potato failure was now all but certain, Trevelyan decided that 'Commissariat operations ought to be discontinued even if the potato does fail'; ...

Page 370. ...Trevelyan informed Twistleton that Treasury grants to distressed Irish unions were to cease. ... A few weeks later Twistleton was informed that there would be no issue of condemned and unwanted Ordnance clothing to Irish workhouses, as there had been last winter. 'It is a great object not to revive the habit of dependence on Government aid,' wrote Trevelyan, and to encourage independence further he stopped feeding destitute children, in spite of Lord John Russell's pledge, and wrote informing applicants that the British Association's funds were now exhausted and the Government could do nothing.

Page 371. ...Charles Wood wrote to Monteagle, '*I am not at all appalled by your tenantry going ... that seems to me to be a necessary part of the process*': larger holdings were essential in Ireland, and holdings could not be enlarged until the number of holders was diminished. Trevelyan agreed. 'I do not know how farms are to be consolidated if small farmers do not emigrate', he wrote, 'and by acting for the purpose of keeping them at home, we should be defeating our own object. We must not complain of what we really want to obtain. If small farmers go, and then landlords are induced to sell portions of their estates to persons who will invest capital, we shall at last arrive at something like a satisfactory settlement of the country.'

Page 375. ... Twistleton told Trevelyan he had thought it better to omit from the Annual Report of the Poor Law Commission (Ireland) any statement as to how much each pauper cost, in case people should say 'we were slowly murdering the peasantry by the scantiness of our relief '. ... The answer was that *Ireland was to be abandoned to Trevelyan's operation-of-natural-causes system.* ... wrote Lord John [Russell],... '*Let us not grant, lend, clothe, etc., any more, and see what that will do*'. ...

Page 380. For Twistleton the rate-in-aid was the last straw, and on March 12 he resigned. 'He thinks,' Clarendon told Lord John Russell on the same day, 'that the destitution here [in Ireland] is so horrible, and the indifference of the House of Commons to it is so manifest, that he is an unfit agent of a policy which must be one of extermination ...Twistleton feels that as Chief Commissioner he is placed in a position ... which no man of honour and humanity can endure.

Page 381. ...Asiatic cholera... In spite of this new blow the

British Government remained adamant—the Irish unions were not to be helped. ... Clarendon now became frantic: ... 'for I don't think there is another legislature in Europe that would disregard such suffering as now exists in the west of Ireland, or *coldly persist in a policy of extermination'*. ...

Page 408. ... after the transfer to the Poor Law in the summer of 1847, the behaviour of the British Government is difficult to defend. Lord John Russell and his advisers, in particular Sir Charles Wood and Trevelyan, were aware of the state of the Irish Poor Law. ... even breaking Lord John Russell's pledge to feed the starving children.

Page 411. How many people died in the famine will never precisely be known. ...*a loss of at least 2 ½ million persons had taken place.*

Page 415. Trevelyan's work in the Irish famine for which in April 1848 he was made Sir Charles Trevelyan, K.C.B., ...Periodic famines occurred during his Indian service. ...

From Sean Burke, *Genocide Complaint Against Britain for the "Potato Famine,"* International Human Rights Law Paper, Spring Semester 2001 (March 14, 2002).

Pages 20-21. On May 30, 1997, Prime Minister Tony Blair sent an official press release of the British Government to be read at the Great Famine Event in Cork, Ireland. The relevant portion of the text provides:

> The Famine was a defining event in the history of Ireland and of Britain. It has left deep scars. That one million people should have died in what was then part of the richest and most powerful nation in the world is something that still causes pain as we reflect on it today. Those who governed at the time failed their people through standing by while a crop failure turned into a massive human tragedy. We must not forget such a dreadful event.

> Toby Harnden, *Blair Apologizes to Ireland for the Potato Famine*, International News, Jun. 2, 1997.

Page 24. Trevelyan's correspondence throughout this period acts as shocking evidence proving that he acted with intent and design to use the Potato Famine as a means to restructure Ireland by exterminating or by forcing its poor to emigrate. Thus, the Irish population would be brought to a more "satisfactory level." Kinealy, *A Death-Dealing Famine*, at 126.

Page 25. Trevelyan's racist feelings toward the Irish, and specifically the Catholics, are evident prior to and throughout the Famine. While he himself had Irish roots, he considered himself to be a "reformed Celt." Charles Trevelyan, *The Irish Crisis*, (1848) (originally published in the *Edinburgh Review* anonymously) (originally cited in Kinealy, *Death*, at 58). These familial roots did not prevent Trevelyan from believing "The great evil with which we have to contend is not the physical evil of the famine, but the moral evil of the selfish, perverse and truculent character of the people." Charles Trevelyan to Jones, December 2, 1846, P.L.B. Vol. X (as cited in Cecil Woodham-Smith, *The Great Hunger*, at 156). In addition to being inferior in character to the British, Trevelyan believed that the Irish were inferior in the eyes of God. He stated that the Famine was "the judgement of God on an indolent and unself-reliant people" in what may have been an attempt to justify why he was not doing more to relieve the pains of the Irish people. Charles Trevelyan, *The Irish Crisis*, (originally cited in Kinealy, *Death*, at 4). This moralistic, anti-Catholic, providential view was held not only by Trevelyan, but was common among the public and other government officials, including Charles Wood.

Page 25. In 1847, anonymously and without previous authority, Trevelyan wrote a letter that was published in *The Times*. Kinealy, *Death*, at 121. This letter purported to lay out the pattern of relief for the coming year. The London Times, Oct. 12, 1847. This goal of this policy was to change Ireland "from an idle, barbarous isolated potato cultivation, to corn cultivation", but importantly this must include "capital and a new class of men." *Id*.

Pages 26-27. Because Trevelyan believed that the Famine was an act of God condemning the Irish, he felt that they and not England were responsible for its abatement. Therefore, he designed British policy to make the Irish people choose between "a lamentable loss of life of the lower classes, and the temporary distress of those classes whose duty it is to give employment to able bodied poor and gratuitous relief for the impotent poor." Kinealy, *This Great Calamity*, at 229. Nevertheless, in his personal writing Trevelyan acknowledged and accurately predicted that if the government did not provide minimal relief "the deaths would shock the world and be an eternal blot on the nation, and the government will be blamed." *Private Report by Trevelyan*, PROL T.64.336A. (1849)(originally cited in Kinealy, *Calamity*, at 249). Consistent with his providential view of the Famine, he compared the poor in Ireland to the Bible's prodigal son, but he was not about to kill the fatted calf for them. *Id.* On the contrary, "the workhouse and one pound of meal per day" was their sentence, if they were lucky enough to get that. *Id.* One gains keen insight into Trevelyan's theory of Famine relief by examining the following statement:

The owners and holders of land in these districts had permitted or encouraged the growth of the *excessive population* which depended upon the precarious potato and they alone had it in their power to restore society to a safe and healthy state. Trevelyan, Irish Crisis, at 79 (emphasis added).

Page 28-29. ...Later, in a letter to Lord Clarendon, Wood defended the miserly English relief policies by claiming that without "a purgatory of misery and starvation, I cannot see how Ireland is to emerge into anything approaching either quiet or prosperity." Wood to Clarendon, *Hickleton Papers*, Jul. 23, 1847.

Page 29-30. Wood saw eviction as another important tool of change. When evictions became rampant in Ireland, Wood and Trevelyan kept prodding the Poor Law Commissioners to pressure landlords to pay their poor rates because that would "lead to some emigrating...what we really want to obtain is a clearance of small farmers." Wood to Poor Law Commissioners, T.64366.A, Sept. 9, 1848 (originally cited in Kinealy, *Calamity*, at 315).

Page 30-31... Clarendon did not come to Ireland as a friend, and he especially disliked Catholics. Indeed, he even stated that "'the departure of thousands of papist Celts must be a blessing to the country they quit' and he was particularly pleased to note that 'Some English and Scottish settlers have arrived.'" Kinealy, *Death*, at 146. He, like many of the Whig party, believed that the worst of the Famine had passed and was not disturbed when blight reappeared in 1847. Kinealy, *Death*, at 119-20. Clarendon replied that if the crop returned in abundance "both the people and the landlords would rely on them as much as ever, and the experience of the last year would go for absolutely nothing." Clarendon to Wood, Jul.12, 1848 (originally cited in Kinealy, *Death*, at 175). He confidently predicted:

In the next two years there will be a grand struggle and the government of Ireland will be a painful thankless task, but I am convinced that the failure of the potatoes and the establishment of the Poor Law will eventually be the salvation of the country- the first will prevent the land from being used as it hitherto has been. Clarendon to Wood, Jul.15, 1848 (originally cited in

Kinealy, *Death*, at 175).

Page 31. As the Famine and misery dragged on and no relief came, Clarendon again wrote to Russell:

> ...it is enough to drive one mad, day after day, to read the appeals that are made and meet them all with a negative... At Westport, and other places in Mayo, they have not a shilling to make preparations for the cholera, but no assistance can be given, and there is no credit for anything, as all our contractors are ruined. Surely this is a state of things to justify you asking the House of Commons for an advance, for I don't think there is another legislature in Europe that would disregard such suffering as now exists in the west of Ireland, or coldly persist in a *policy of extermination*. Clarendon to Russell, *Irish Letter-Books*, Apr. 28, 1849 (originally cited in Kinealy, *Death,* at 138) (emphasis added).

Page 31. In 1847, after seeing the devastation known as 'Black 47' a defeated Lord Clarendon placed blame:

> C. Wood backed by Grey, and relying upon arguments (or rather Trevelyanisms) that are no more applicable to Ireland than to Loo Choo, affirmed that the right thing to do was to do nothing—they have prevailed and you see what a fix we are in. Clarendon to Duke of Bedford, *Clarendon Papers*, Feb. 16, 1849 (originally cited in Kinealy, *Death*, at 138).

Page 32-33. ... In one Request, Twistleton said if people knew of the degradation in Ireland they "might say that we are slowly murdering the peasantry by the scantiness of relief." Twistleton to Trevelyan, PROL T.64.366.A, Jan. 21, 1849 (originally cited in Kinealy, *Death*, at 130).

Page 33. Helping to explain Twistleton's resignation, Lord Clarendon wrote to Lord Russell that "He thinks that the destitution here is so horrible, and the indifference of the House of Commons to it is so manifest, that he is an unfit agent of a policy that must be one of extermination." Clarendon to Russell, *Clarendon Letterbooks,* Mar. 12, 1849 (originally cited in Kinealy, *Death*, at 145).

Page 34. ... In 1849, Twistleton testified in front of a Select Committee on the Irish Poor Law. Evidence of Edward Twistleton, *Select Committee on the Irish Poor Law*, 1849, xvi, 699-714. He declared that:

> comparatively trifling sums were required for Britain

to spare itself the deep disgrace of permitting its miserable fellow subjects to die of starvation. I wish to leave distinctly on the record that, from want of sufficient food, many persons in these Unions are at present dying or wasting away; and, at the same time, it is quite possible for this country to prevent the occurrence there of any death from starvation, by the advance of a few hundred pounds. *Id.*

Page 34. ... Nassau Senior, a respected economics professor at Oxford and a leading critic of the Royal Commission that studied poverty in Ireland, stated that the Famine in Ireland "would not kill more than one million people, and that would scarcely be enough to do any good." Michael & Thomas Gallagher, *Paddy's Lament* 84 (1982) (quoting Senior).

Pages 34-35. Sir Randolph Routh held the position of Chief Commissioner in charge of relief operations in 1845-6. He, too, felt the Famine was an opportunity for England rather than a crisis:

The little industry called for to rear the potato, and its prolific growth, leave the people to indolence and all kinds of vice, which habitual labor and a higher order of food would prevent. I think it is very probable that we may derive much advantage from this present calamity. Sir Randolph Routh to Charles Trevelyan, *Correspondence Explanatory of the measures adopted by Her Majesty's Government for the relief of distress arising from the failure of the potato crop in Ireland,* 139 Apr. 1, 1846 (originally cited in Kinealy, *Death,* at 83).

Page 35. Finally, a post-Famine Census Commission in a congratulatory tone reported:

In conclusion, we feel it will be gratifying to your Excellency to find that although the population has been diminished in so remarkable a manner by famine, disease and emigration between 1845 and 1851, and has been since decreasing, the results of the Irish census of 1851 are, on the whole, satisfactory, demonstrating as they do the general advancement of the country. Kinealy, *Calamity,* at 296.

Page 45. ... This period where there was no relief saw the rise of mortality in many districts. Kinealy, *Calamity*, at 102. A Grand Jury in Kerry remarked that this delay was a 'death warrant' for the poor. *The Times,* Mar. 24, 1847 (originally cited in Kinealy, *Death,* at

102). Rather than showing some flexibility and not leaving an area without relief of any type, the Treasury felt it was better "to incur partial present inconvenience, than be the means of introducing measures productive of eventual injury to the community." Treasury Minute, First Report of the Relief Commissioners, Mar. 10, 1847 (originally cited in Kinealy, *Death*, at 102).

Pages 51-52. ... To further discourage persons who were not truly destitute from taking advantage of the largesse of the Poor Law, hard labor was required of any able-bodied person who received benefits. Kinealy, *Calamity*, at 199.

The work assigned was to be:

as repulsive as possible consistent with humanity, that is, that paupers would rather do the work than 'starve' but that they should rather employ themselves in doing any other kind of work elsewhere. ... Twistleton to Trevelyan, PROL T.64.370. C/4, Feb.27, 1848 (originally cited in Kinealy, *Calamity*, at 200).

The task decided upon was stone-breaking. Stone-breaking met the criteria above and did not interfere with work found on the free market. Kinealy, *Calamity*, at 200. It was an easily measurable task that was hated by the workers who had to break stones for eight and ten hours to eat. *Id.*

Pages 52-53. ... After battling hunger and debt for three years, the people in the distressed unions were at "nearly the lowest point of squalor and want at which human beings can exist." Commissioners to Grey, *Distressed Unions*, 26 (Jan.2, 1849) (originally cited in Kinealy, *Calamity*, at 239). Still the Treasury continued to withhold money at their expense.

Page 53. Trevelyan, knowing that this would further stress the Poor Law and require more advances, asked the Society of Friends to remain in Ireland. Kinealy, *Calamity*, at 160. Refusing, they told Trevelyan that more drastic measures were needed and their staying was "like giving a criminal a long day." *Id.* A third year of suffering and devastating hunger was on tap for the Irish.

Page 54. In 1850, [the Rate-in-Aid Act] prompted George Poulett Scrope an investigatory body was set up to analyze the implementation of the Poor Law in the Kilrush Union. Kinealy, *Calamity*, at 288. This investigation was critical of the local landlords and their own government. *Id.* at 290. In conclusion it stated:

Whether as regards the plain principles of humanity, or the literal text and admitted principle of the Poor Law of 1847, a neglect or [sic] public duty has occurred and has occasioned a state of things disgraceful to a civilized age and country, for which some authority ought to be held responsible, and would long since have been held responsible had these things occurred in any union in England. *Report of the Select Committee Appointed to Enquire into the Administration of the Poor Law in the Kilrush Union since 19 September 1848,* xii (1850) (originally cited in Kinealy, *Calamity,* at 290).

Pages 57-58. Unfortunately for the Irish, not enough British politicians were concerned with the harsh evictions. "When the Poor Law Commissioner complained of the hardship resulting from these clearances, Trevelyan responded that only through this process would Ireland 'at last arrive at something like a satisfactory settlement of the country.'" Kinealy, *Death,* at 126. The House of Commons was told that "Ejectment is tantamount to a sentence of death by slow torture." George Poulett Scrope, House of Commons, Apr. 27, 1846, Hansard, 1077 vol. 85 (originally cited in *Great Hunger,* at 32). Eventually, things got so bad that the Parliament passed the Crime and Outrage Bill. Kinealy, *Death,* at 127. This measure was not supposed to stop the underlying problem of evictions, but to keep law and order after the evictions. Kinealy, *Calamity,* at 219.

Pages 58-59. ... The Gregory Clause took its name from the person who introduced it, William Gregory an MP for Dublin and landlord in Galway. Kinealy, *Death,* at 123. When confronted with the fact that this clause would destroy the class of small farmers, he replied that "he did not see of what use such small farmers could possibly be." Canon John O'Rourke, *The Great Irish Famine,* 171 (1874) (quoting Gregory) (originally cited in Kinealy, *Death,* at 123). These sentiments were echoed by other MPs like Lord Palmerston, also an Irish landowner, who stated:

It is useless to describe the truth that any great improvement in the social system in Ireland must be founded upon an extensive change in the present state of agrarian occupation, and that this change necessarily implies a long, continued and systematic ejection of small landholders and of squatting cottiers. Memorial by Lord Palmerston to Russell, *Russell Correspondence*, at 225 (originally cited in Kinealy, *Death,* at 123).

Page 62. Even though direct government financing of emigration was relatively low, the idea of was encouraged and embraced by the likes of Wood and Trevelyan on down to the workhouse guardians. Kinealy, *Calamity*, at 311. It was seen by all as a solution to the stress being placed on the Poor Law and a way to reduce Ireland's population. *Id.* In denying one request by the Poor Law Commissioners for money, Trevelyan explained:

I do not know how farms are to be consolidated if small farmers do not emigrate, and by acting for the purpose of keeping them at home, we should be defaulting at our own object. We must not complain of what we really want to obtain. If small farmers go, and their landlords are reduced to sell portions of their estates to persons who will invest capital, we shall arrive at last at something like a satisfactory settlement of this country. Trevelyan to Twistleton, PROL T.64.370. B/1, Sept. 14, 1848 (originally cited in Kinealy, *Calamity,* at 414).

Similarly, Wood stated that if poor rates are continued to be collected diligently "the pressure will lead to some emigrating... what we really want to obtain is a clearance of small farmers. Wood to Poor Law Commissioners, T.64.366.A, Sept. 9, 1848 (originally cited in Kinealy, *Calamity,* at 315).

Page 67. ... Things in Ireland were so bad that *The Times* predicted that "in a few years more a Celtic Irishman will be as rare in Connemara as the Red Indian on the shores of Manhattan." Donal A. Kerr, *A Nation of Beggars? Priests, People and Politics Famine Ireland 1846-52,* 297 (1994) (quoting *The Times*).

Pages 67-68. These stories and the high loss of life were known to the people in charge of the relief. Lord George Bentinck assures us of that:

They know the people have been dying by their thousands and I dare them to enquire what has been the number of those who have died through their mismanagement, by their policies of free trade. Yes, free trade in the lives of the Irish people. *Letter to Mr. Monsell of Limerick Assizes, Northern Whig,* Apr. 1, 1847 (originally cited in Kinealy, *Calamity,* at 169).

Page 74. In 1848, A Cork City Councilor named Brady explained to his audience that the British Prime Minister had:

Violated every pledge previously made on arriving at place and power...a million and a half Irish people perished, were smitten and offered up as a holocaust, whose blood ascended to the throne of God for redress..., but the pity was that the minister was permitted to act so with impunity. Irish Famine Curriculum Committee, The Great Irish Famine 105 (1996).

Conclusion

There will never be any statute of limitations for Britain's genocide against the Irish. And according to the international law doctrine known as "the legal continuity of states" (i.e., "state continuity") all of this historical evidence against Britain for genocide still applies today and binds and self-incriminates Britain now as a matter of contemporary international law. The State known today as Britain has been continuously in legal existence since it was founded in 1066. Therefore, Britain today is legally responsible for all the mass atrocities that it has inflicted upon the Irish as well as upon all the other oppressed peoples around the world since the so-called Battle of Hastings after the Norman invasion and conquest of England. I would be more than happy to consult with their respective lawyers on filing genocide charges against Britain at the World Court on behalf of their clients too.

It is way beyond historical time to bring Britain to justice before it exterminates other races of people yet again, and again, and again as Perfidious Albion has serially and shamelessly done throughout the past millennium—starting with the Irish, and now most recently in Iraq, Afghanistan, and Libya. Who is the next victim on Britain's genocidal hit-list? What can humanity do to stop them? Bringing Britain to legal account for its genocide against the Irish would be an excellent place to start!

In this regard, on May 30, 1997 British Prime Minister Tony Blair issued an official Message on behalf of Britain for reading at a Great Famine event held in County Cork, Ireland.[8] For the purposes of legal analysis here, the relevant part of this Message is as follows:

> ...The Famine was a defining event in the history of Ireland and of Britain. It has left deep scars. That one million people should have died in what was then part of the richest and most powerful nation in the world is something that still causes pain as we reflect on it today. Those who governed in London at the time failed their people through standing by while a crop failure turned into a massive human tragedy. We must not forget such a dreadful event. ...

The news media misleadingly portrayed this Message as a British "apology" for the "Irish Potato Famine." It was nothing of the sort! At best, this very carefully and cleverly drafted Message can be construed to imply that British government officials at the time were no more than somewhat negligent in their handling of a natural catastrophe similar to the recent tsunami in Japan, or Hurricane Katrina, or the earthquake in Haiti, etc. Blair's implication was that no one was legally—let alone criminally—responsible for much of anything at all.

To the contrary, it is the responsibility of tens of millions of Irish People all over the world to categorically reject Britain's self-exonerating description of the Irish Hecatomb. The Irish Diaspora must organize an international Campaign for Reparations for Genocide against Britain along the lines of what the Jewish People have quite successfully done against Germany.[9] Monetary damages can never atone for the genocidal catastrophe that Britain inflicted upon Ireland and the Irish. But it is the principle that counts. And the satisfaction of this principle might then produce genuine healing between the British and the Irish. No one is wallowing in victimhood. But peace can only be built upon justice.

ENDNOTES

1   *See* Irish Echo, Feb.26-March 4, 1997, at page 7 for the list of 125 distinguished signatories.

2   *See* Francis A. Boyle, *Trying to Stop Aggressive War and Genocide Against the People and the Republic of Bosnia and Herzegovina* in my The Palestinian Right of Return under International Law 105-33 (2011) and in my The Tamil Genocide by Sri Lanka 71-95 (2010). *See also* Francis A. Boyle, The Bosnian People Charge Genocide! (1996).

3   *See* Francis A. Boyle, *Is Bosnia the End of the Road for the United Nations?*, 6 Periodica Islamica, No. 2 at 45 (1996).

4   *See* U.N. Doc. A/48/659-S/26806, 47 U.N.Y.B. 465 (1993).

5   Steve Doughty, *Irish Lawyer Joins Fight As Muslims Cry "Murder,"* Daily Mail, November 17, 1993.

6   *See U.N. Genocide Charge Puts Any Bosnia Role in Doubt,* Daily Telegraph, November 17, 1993.

7   *Case Concerning the Application of the Convention on the Prevention and Punishment of the Crime of Genocide (Bosnia and Herzegovina v. Serbia and Montenegro),* International Court of Justice, Judgment, 26 February 2007 (merits).

8   Sarah Lyall, *Past as Prologue: Blair Faults Britain in Irish Potato Blight,* New York Times, June 3, 1997.

9   *See, e.g.,* Ben Ferencz, Less Than Slaves: Jewish Forced Labor and the Quest for Compensation (1979); Scott Leckie, Housing, Land and Property Restitution Rights of Refugees and Displaced Persons (2007).

CHAPTER TWO

THE DECOLONIZATION
OF NORTHERN IRELAND

It is only appropriate that a book promoting and advancing United Ireland detail precisely the obligation of Britain to decolonize Northern Ireland as required by international law in order to bring about United Ireland. My article "The Decolonization of Northern Ireland" undertook this task in 1994, and appeared in Volume 4 of the Asian Yearbook of International Law. *As pointed out in its Postscript, pursuant to the terms of the December 15, 1993* **Downing Street Declaration on Northern Ireland** *concluded between the British and Irish governments, Britain thereby formally and publicly acknowledged the right of the Irish People living on the Island of Ireland to exercise their right of self-determination. This is the exact same result decreed by the seminal United Nations Decolonization Resolution of 1960.*

Then on Feb. 22, 1995 **A New Framework for Agreement** *was concluded between Ireland and Britain right after the I.R.A. Ceasefire Statement of 31 August 1994. Here, both Britain and Ireland officially recognized and agreed that there are two different peoples living on two different islands—the Irish living on Ireland and the British living on Britain, respectively. And each people is a separate unit for self-determination purposes on each island, respectively. Hence, the Irish People living on the entire Island of Ireland have the right to self-determination. And the British People living on the entire Island of Britain have the right to self-determination. Furthermore, Protestants living in Northern Ireland are not being treated as a separate unit for self-determination purposes. Nor are Protestants living in Northern Ireland being treated as part of the British unit for self-determination purposes. Rather, Protestants living in Northern Ireland are being treated as part of the Irish People living on* *the Island of Ireland, which is the Irish unit for self-determination. These legally agreed upon conclusions by Britain and Ireland are consistent with the analysis set forth in my 1994 scholarly article.*

*Next, to the same effect, came the **Consultative Document on All-Party Talks in the North** that was issued by Britain and Ireland on March 18, 1996. Finally, continuously building upon these previous agreements, Article 1(iv) of the path-breaking 1998 **Good Friday/Belfast Agreement** concluded between Britain and Ireland made this point crystal clear: the parties hereto "affirm that, if in the future, the people of the island of Ireland exercise their right of self-determination on the basis set out in sections (i) and (ii) above to bring about a united Ireland, it will be a binding obligation on both Governments to introduce and support in their respective Parliaments legislation to give effect to that wish..." By means of this language, both Britain and Ireland have recognized and agreed that at the end of the day there will be United Ireland.*

Furthermore, by means of the 1998 Good Friday/Belfast Agreement, Britain and Ireland have knowingly put into motion a political, legal, and economic process that will ineluctably result in United Ireland. Moreover, by means of concluding the 1998 Good Friday/Belfast Agreement, Britain and Ireland have deliberately established what political scientists denominate a "regime"[1] for the purpose of creating United Ireland. It is only a question of time.

Given the current differential demographic trends for Catholics and Protestants in Northern Ireland, the progressive and good-faith implementation of the 1998 Good Friday/Belfast Agreement might require one generation to produce United Ireland. But one generation is only the bat of an eye in the ancient history of the Irish, who are the original, indigenous People of Ireland. The critical point is that by means of concluding the 1998 Good Friday/Belfast Agreement, Britain and Ireland have rendered United Ireland an historical inevitability. The final chapter in this book will set forth some additional recommendations on how to bring forth United Ireland beyond those already suggested in my 1994 article reprinted below.

Introduction

Historically, the British government has been quite successful at defining the situation in Northern Ireland in accordance with its own national self-interests as it sees fit.[2] It has spent an enormous amount of resources on conveying to the world news media why its particular approach to the problem—whatever it might be at that particular moment in time—is the only correct approach.[3] I would submit, however, that there is certainly another way of looking at the situation in Northern

Ireland. That other way of analyzing this conflict is from the perspective of international law, and in particular the United Nations Charter. Therefore, it is my task here to describe what I believe should be the appropriate policy of the world community of states toward the situation in Northern Ireland in accordance with the requirements of international law.

Article 1, paragraph 2 of the United Nations Charter provides that one of the "Purposes" of the United Nations Organization is to develop friendly relations among nations based on respect for the principle of equal rights and self-determination of peoples.[4] This fundamental principle of self-determination for peoples can also be found in the two seminal United Nations Human Rights Covenants of 1966: The International Covenant on Civil and Political Rights, and the International Covenant on Economic, Social, and Cultural Rights.[5] Both of these Covenants have been ratified by the British and Irish governments; and of course both states are parties to the United Nations Charter, as is true for most states of the world community.[6] Thus, both states are in basic agreement upon the fundamentality of the principle of self-determination of peoples and its integral connection to the maintenance of international peace and security.[7] The principle of self-determination of peoples has been a basic norm of international law and of world politics since it was first proclaimed by President Woodrow Wilson in his famous Fourteen Points Address of 1918.[8]

The Colonial Status of Northern Ireland

In 1960 the United Nations General Assembly took a monumental step toward implementing the right of self-determination of peoples throughout the world by means of adopting its Declaration on the Granting of Independence to Colonial Countries and Territories, Resolution 1514(XV) of 14 December.[9] I will not bother to discuss all of its provisions here, but I would like to mention its most salient features. In the Preamble, the General Assembly "solemnly proclaims the necessity of bringing to speedy and unconditional end colonialism in all its forms and manifestations."[10] It also declares in paragraph 1 that: "The subjection of peoples to alien subjugation, domination and exploitation constitutes a denial of fundamental human rights, is contrary to the Charter of the United Nations, and is an impediment to the promotion of world peace and cooperation."[11] Likewise paragraph 4 provides that all armed action or repressive measures of all kinds directed against dependent peoples shall cease in order to enable them to exercise peacefully and freely their right to complete independence, and the integrity of their national territories shall be respected.[12]

Next, paragraph 5 requires that immediate steps shall be taken in trust and non-self-governing territories or all other territories which have not yet attained independence to transfer all powers to the peoples of those territories without any conditions or reservations, etc.[13] Nevertheless, paragraph 6 makes it clear that the implementation of paragraph 5 cannot be undertaken in a manner that would aim "at the partial or total disruption of the national unity and the territorial integrity of a country."[14] To quote from the exact language of paragraph 6: "Any attempt aimed at the partial or total disruption of the national unity and the territorial integrity of a country is incompatible with the purposes and principles of the Charter of the United Nations."[15]

In addition, this basic principle of international law mandating the equal rights and self-determination of peoples has likewise been enshrined in the Declaration on Principles of International Law Concerning Friendly Relations and Cooperation Among States in Accordance with the Charter of the United Nations, which was adopted by the U.N. General Assembly on October 24, 1970 as Resolution 2625 (XXV).[16] In particular therein can be found the injunction: "Every state shall refrain from any action aimed at the partial or total disruption of the national unity and territorial integrity of any other state or country."[17] This Declaration was adopted by the General Assembly as a "consensus resolution," which means that the British government did not dissent from it.[18] Finally, this particular resolution was also treated by the International Court of Justice as enunciating rules of customary international law in its 1986 Judgment on the merits in the case of *Nicaragua v. United States*.[19]

Pursuant to the aforementioned Decolonization Resolution and the Declaration of Principles Resolution, the continuing partition of Ireland constitutes an illegal partial disruption of the national unity and territorial integrity of the state of Ireland, which violates the terms of the United Nations Charter and, in particular, the aforementioned right of the Irish People to self-determination.[20] From the perspective of international law, therefore, the entity which the British government calls "Northern Ireland" is in fact and in law a "colony" as that term has been classically defined.[21] I submit that this is precisely how the world community of states must proceed to think about the situation in Northern Ireland if it is to make any sense of what is going on over there, and more importantly, to determine what should be done to solve the problems of Northern Ireland.

The U.N. Decolonization of Northern Ireland

According to this U.N. Decolonization Resolution of 1960 and the two U.N. Human Rights Covenants of 1966, the British government is under an absolute international legal obligation to decolonize Northern

Ireland in cooperation with the United Nations as expeditiously as possible and in the process to restore the territorial integrity of the whole state of Ireland.[22] In other words, Britain must remove the last vestiges of the colonial occupation it had imposed upon Ireland as a result of its so-called Treaty of Partition of 1921.[23] Here the United Nations Organization as a whole, including the Trusteeship Council, the Special Committee on Decolonization, as well as the United Nations General Assembly, have had an enormous amount of quite successful practice with respect to obtaining the peaceful decolonization of occupied territories by former colonial imperial powers—especially Great Britain—around the world.[24] It is to this wealth of experience, then, that the world community of states must look in order to obtain some useful precedents that could be applied to the peaceful resolution of the situation in Northern Ireland.

In this regard, when the British government sent troops to Northern Ireland in 1969 the Irish government sought to raise the question of "the six counties of Northern Ireland" before the United Nations Security Council, appealing for the "dispatch to the area of a United Nations peacekeeping force."[25] Due to threat of a British veto, however, the Security Council adjourned without taking a decision on whether or not to adopt the agenda.[26] The Security Council never again considered the question.

Nevertheless, Irish Ambassador Cremin submitted an Explanatory Memorandum on the situation in Northern Ireland to the General Committee of the U.N. General Assembly requesting that this topic be included on the Assembly's agenda.[27] Following the proposal of Nigeria, the General Committee decided to defer a decision on whether or not to recommend the inclusion of this agenda item.[28] Since that time, however, representatives of successive Irish governments have reiterated the right to national reunification in addresses to the U.N. General Assembly.[29]

The situation in Northern Ireland clearly constitutes a threat to the maintenance of international peace and security. Therefore the United Nations Security Council has all the authorization it needs to act in whatever manner it deems fit to deal with Northern Ireland since the Security Council has "primary responsibility for the maintenance of international peace and security" under Charter article 24.[30] Hence, some day a majority of nine members of the Security Council could decide to send a U.N. peacekeeping force to Northern Ireland. In this fashion, the decolonization of Northern Ireland could be initiated by the withdrawal of British troops and the emplacement of a U.N. peacekeeping force in their stead on a transitional basis. Witness, for example, the recently successful decolonization of Namibia (formerly Southwest Africa) under the auspices of a United Nations peacekeeping force (i.e., the U.N. Transition Assistance Group) organized under the authority of the United Nations Security Council.

To be sure, it has always been the case in United Nations practice that a peacekeeping force has never been dispatched against the will of the government with military control over the territory involved, irrespective of whether that government was legally entitled to be there or not.[31] So implementation of this U.N. plan would ultimately depend upon the British and Irish governments reaching some prior agreement on the peaceful decolonization of Northern Ireland and the reunification of Ireland as required by international law. Therefore, it should be a primary goal of the world community of states to encourage the British government (1) to publicly endorse the principle of decolonization for Northern Ireland, as well as (2) to negotiate in good faith with the Irish government on a reunification treaty. Thereafter, both states should work in cooperation with the U.N. Security Council, the U.N. Secretary General, and a U.N. peacekeeping force to accomplish these objectives.

The Protection of Human Rights in Northern Ireland

At this preliminary point in the analysis, no point would be served by speculating about what type of United Irish State might ultimately emerge from these reunification talks. It could be a confederal state organized along the lines of Switzerland, or a federal state consisting of two parts, or a unitary state, etc.[32] The selection of any one of these alternatives (or some other) would be for all of the people living on the Island of Ireland—whether Protestant or Catholic—to determine, subject to the final approval of the United Nations Organization.

From an international law perspective, however, the most important part of these reunification negotiations to be considered would be the protection of the basic fundamental human rights of Protestants living in Northern Ireland and the firm establishment of their right to continue to live and practice their religion as they see fit. The ability to do this has been made immeasurably easier by the fact that both the British government and the Irish government are parties to the two aforementioned United Nations Human Rights Covenants of 1966.[33] The British government signed both U.N. Covenants in 1968 and ratified them in 1976.[34] The Irish government signed both in 1973 and has recently ratified them.[35] Moreover, Ireland has also become a party to the 1966 Optional Protocol to the International Covenant on Civil and Political Rights giving competence to the United Nations Human Rights Committee to receive and consider communications from individuals claiming to be victims of a violation by that state party of any of the rights set forth in the Covenant.[36]

In addition, both Britain and Ireland are parties to the European Convention on Human Rights.[37] And it would be necessary for a United Ireland to adopt domestic implementing legislation for all three[38] of these seminal international human rights treaties as well.[39] In this manner, any Protestant residing in a United Ireland who believed that his or her rights had been abridged on grounds of religion or nationality would have direct and immediate access to a court of law on the basis of any one or more of these three treaties and their respective implementing legislation.

In all fairness, I should point out that this is not the case today for Irish Catholics living in Northern Ireland who allege discrimination against them on the grounds of religion or nationality. The British government has been quite clever at signing various human rights treaties, but then derogating from their provisions by proclaiming a public emergency with respect to Northern Ireland.[40] In addition, the British government has not adopted domestic implementing legislation for these three human rights conventions.[41*] This then prevents Irish Catholics living in Northern Ireland from going into court and pleading a cause of action directly under these treaties in order to strike down the widespread discriminatory practices against Irish Catholics currently existing there. Moreover, even large segments of the British People themselves continue to lament the fact that they do not have a domestic constitutional equivalent of a Bill of Rights.

But just because the British government has tolerated and condoned widespread discrimination against Irish Catholics in Northern Ireland would provide absolutely no good reason for the Irish government to do the same against Protestants in a decolonized state of United Ireland.[42] Indeed, it has been the gross violation of the fundamental human rights of Irish Catholics in Northern Ireland—despite these solemn international treaty commitments to the contrary—that has produced the violent response by the Provisional Irish Republican Army to the British occupation army, regime, and practices.[43] Hence, the world community of states must understand that the violence committed by the Irish paramilitary parties to this international conflict can be directly attributed to the continuation of the illegal British colony on the Island of Ireland, as well as to the concomitant gross violation of fundamental human rights perpetrated by the British occupation forces upon Irish Catholics.[44] For this reason, then, the Provisional I.R.A. must be fit within the broader political, economic and legal context of an anti-colonial war.[45]

---

* The British Parliament later adopted the Human Rights Act of 1998 that incorporated the European Convention on Human Rights into domestic law.

These phenomena are similar to those found in most other anti-colonial wars around the world where the indigenous people have risen up to throw off their colonial oppressors. In such cases, it has proven to be standard operating procedure for the colonial occupation power to play off one group of indigenous people against another, or settlers against the indigenous people; and then for the colonial power to attempt to portray itself as the "peacekeeper" between the contending factions in order to justify the continuation of its colonial occupation.[46] This is precisely what has happened in Northern Ireland.[47] Despite pro-British news media accounts to the contrary, it is the continued presence of the British colonial army, occupation regime, and their military practices in Northern Ireland that have always been the primary source of bloodshed and violence there.[48]

Citizenship, Nationality, and Residence

Another protection that could be afforded to Protestants in Northern Ireland would be for them to be able to retain their British citizenship while living in a United Ireland. They would also retain their British passports and could have the British Parliament guarantee as a matter of domestic law their right (and that of their descendants) to reside in Britain forever. Moreover, the British Parliament could enact legislation to permit British citizens living in a United Ireland to vote in British elections by means of an absentee ballot.

Protestants living in Northern Ireland should be entitled to claim citizenship in a United Ireland and thus become dual nationals if they so desire. On the other hand, Northern Ireland Protestants (and their descendants) should not be forced to accept Irish citizenship or nationality in a United Ireland if they do not want to. Nevertheless, such individuals (and their descendants) should still retain their right of permanent residence in a United Irish State.

To be sure, if such individuals choose to remain living in United Ireland as exclusively British citizens, then they would be bound to obey the laws of a United Ireland—just as is true for permanent resident aliens in any other country. Nevertheless, they would still be entitled to invoke all the protections of the international and domestic human rights regime outlined above. Moreover, since they are currently residents on the Island of Ireland, such individuals should have the basic right to participate in the drafting of a new Constitution for a United Irish State that would contain within itself a Bill of Rights protecting all the people who live in Ireland irrespective of citizenship and nationality, let alone religion.

Furthermore, under that new Constitution, such individuals should be permitted to vote in whatever type of Irish elections they so desire on the basis of their qualifications as permanent residents in United Ireland. In this way, communities in today's Northern Ireland that consist of a majority of Protestants could continue to maintain majority political control over local, municipal, and county-wide political bodies in United Ireland, subject to the non-discrimination regime mentioned above. Indeed, the new Irish Constitution should accord such permanent residents of a United Ireland all of the legal, political, and constitutional rights of Irish citizens without any distinction. These rights should include those of full and equal participation in voting, law-making, governance, administration, adjudication, public office-holding, education, etc. Of course such individuals would remain free to exercise or not exercise any one or more of these rights guaranteed to them by the new Irish Constitution. But for all functional purposes, there should be no constitutional or legal distinctions whatsoever drawn between these Protestant permanent resident aliens and citizens in a United State of Ireland.

No point would be served by continuing to spell out the multifarious constitutional, legal, political, and human rights protections that could be designed for Protestants—with their active participation—who would be living in a United Irish State. Suffice it to say here that enormous progress can be made in this direction by breaking down and distinguishing the rights pertaining to (1) citizenship; (2) nationality; (3) residence; (4) voting; and (5) governance in a United Ireland. Fortunately, all these questions will be made incredibly easy to handle and therefore quite flexible to negotiate because both Great Britain and Ireland are members of the European Union (E.U.)— formerly the European Economic Community (E.E.C.) -- and thus bound by the various protections and privileges afforded citizens of E.U. member states without discrimination.[49] Admittedly, there might be a few hard-line Unionists in Northern Ireland who would refuse to live in a United Ireland even with exclusive British citizenship; a British passport; the rights to vote in both British and Irish elections; the right to hold any public office in a United Ireland; and the ultimate right of permanent residence for themselves and their descendants in Great Britain, etc. But I suspect that number would be very small. Such a small number of individuals should not be enabled to stand in the way of finally establishing a definitive peace between the British People and the Irish People. Such irreconcilable Unionists should be given the option of emigration to Britain if they so desire, with relocation assistance provided and full compensation to be paid for any property interests they might decide to relinquish in Northern Ireland. I suspect that number would be even smaller.

Self-determination for the Peoples of Ireland and Britain

This observation brings the analysis to the heart of the British government's claim that it is really in Northern Ireland to protect the right of such irreconcilable Unionists to self-determination.[50] I find that argument to strain credulity. At one time or another, the British government has invaded, occupied and exploited over one-quarter of the known world community of states and peoples during the course of modern history, including substantial sections of Asia, Africa, the Middle East, and North America.[51] Yet now it is portraying itself as the upholder of the principle of national self-determination in Northern Ireland in order to justify its control over one of its last remaining colonial enclaves around the world. Yet, by comparison, in Hong Kong the world community of states saw the British government turn over five and one-half million people to the Communist [dictatorship] government in Beijing with the stroke of a pen—against their wishes and without even bothering to consult them.[52] So much for the British government's reputed concern for the principle of national self-determination.

With respect to Northern Ireland, under international law the principle of self-determination of *peoples* appropriately applies to the entire British People, not a small group of irreconcilable Unionists. In this regard, public opinion polls have repeatedly shown that only 25% of the British People want to remain in Northern Ireland.[53] It seems to me that the wishes of this substantial majority of the British People should—and ultimately will—be respected. For reasons explained more fully below, it is only a question of time before the British government will as a matter of fact and of law decolonize Northern Ireland.

As for those irreconcilable Unionists who are unwilling to live as Britons in a United Ireland under any circumstance, then of course they should be free to emigrate to Britain. If they do not want to remain British in a United Ireland, then by all means they should be permitted to be British in Britain. This option would fully implement whatever their self-proclaimed right of self-determination means, as well as the rights to peace and self-determination for everyone else involved in this conflict—the entirety of the British People and the entirety of the Irish People. The U.N. principle of equal rights and self-determination of *peoples* requires one and only one state for the British People (i.e., Great Britain) and one and only one state for the Irish People (i.e., Ireland). It does not sanction the continuation of an illegal British colony on the Island of Ireland.

The Anglo-Irish Agreement of 1985

These latter observations bring the analysis directly to the Anglo-Irish Agreement of 1985.[54] It used to be the case that the British government had always argued that the situation in Northern Ireland was a "domestic affair" or a matter of "internal concern" invoking article 2, paragraph 7 of the United Nations Charter prohibiting U.N. intervention "in matters which are essentially within the domestic jurisdiction of any state."[55] This is similar to claims that have always been made by imperial colonial powers trying to keep the international community from dealing with a colonial situation in order to better hold onto the colony. Witness, for example, France's outlandish claim that the colonial situation in Algeria was part of the domestic affairs of France because France had annexed Algeria and treated it as an integral part of Metropolitan France, just like Paris.[56]

Illegal fictions to the contrary, however, Algeria was never part of France. And Northern Ireland has never been part of Great Britain. Northern Ireland has always been an integral part of Ireland.

Note, however, that after the signature of the Anglo-Irish Agreement at Hillsborough on 15 November 1985, the British government can no longer make that specious type of claim.[57] This recent Anglo-Irish Agreement giving the Irish government a voice in all matters relating to Northern Ireland represents the ultimate and definitive British capitulation on this point.[58] Whatever the situation was before the Anglo-Irish Agreement of 1985, thereafter, from the perspective of international law, any British claim that the ultimate legal status of, as well as the entire domestic situation in, Northern Ireland are merely matters of "internal concern," would be completely groundless.[59]

This is because of the famous holding of the Permanent Court of International Justice in the *Tunis-Morocco Nationality Decrees Case* of 1923 to the effect that the moment a state concludes an international agreement on any subject, that subject is no longer a matter of exclusively internal concern but thereafter becomes a matter of international concern.[60] By signing the Anglo-Irish Agreement with respect to Northern Ireland in 1985, the British government knowingly removed the entire legal status of, as well as the internal affairs in, Northern Ireland from its so-called domestic jurisdiction to become a matter of international law and world politics. Indeed, the Anglo-Irish Agreement of 1985 has been duly registered with the United Nations Organization in accordance with U.N. Charter article 102.[61] For this reason alone, that aforementioned U.N. Charter article 2, paragraph 7 prohibition can no longer be applied with respect to Northern Ireland.

Sovereignty over Northern Ireland

Quite obviously, no point would be served by attempting to engage in a detailed technical analysis of the 1985 Anglo-Irish Agreement on an article-by-article basis. Suffice it to say here that this interpretation of the Agreement can be substantiated simply by reference to Section A thereof:[62]

A

STATUS OF NORTHERN IRELAND

ARTICLE 1

The two Governments
- (a) affirm that any change in the status of Northern Ireland would only come about with the consent of a majority of the people of Northern Ireland;
- (b) recognize that the present wish of a majority of the people of Northern Ireland is for no change in the status of Northern Ireland;
- (c) declare that, if in the future a majority of the people of Northern Ireland clearly wish for and formally consent to the establishment of a united Ireland, they will introduce and support in the respective Parliaments legislation to give effect to that wish.

In other words, this international treaty specifically purports to deal with the sovereign legal status of Northern Ireland. Hence, according to the *Tunis-Morrocco Nationality Decrees Case*, the sovereign legal status of Northern Ireland is no longer a matter of exclusive domestic concern with respect to Great Britain alone, but is now also officially and legally proclaimed to be the concern of Ireland as well. For that reason, Northern Ireland also becomes the concern of the entire world community of states, including the United Nations Organization and the European Union, *inter alia*.

Furthermore, by means of this treaty provision alone, the British government has effectively abandoned its claim to exercise exclusive sovereign control over Northern Ireland. The claim that a matter falls within the "domestic affairs" of a state is another way of saying that the matter involves a question of that state's "sovereignty." By definition, "domestic affairs" are a question of "state sovereignty," and "state sovereignty" means (in part) a state's exclusive control over its "domestic affairs." Under basic principles of international law, one state's conclusion of an international treaty on a matter of its alleged "domestic affairs" with another state formally removes that subject matter from the exclusive sovereign control of the first state and endows the second state with the right to act upon that subject matter. In this case, the Anglo-Irish Agreement dealt explicitly with the sovereign "STATUS OF NORTHERN IRELAND" as both a juridical and a territorial entity, respectively.

Northern Ireland vs. New Mexico

If the British government truly believed that Northern Ireland was subject to its exclusive sovereign control, then it never would have concluded a treaty with Ireland over the sovereign legal status of Northern Ireland. Here a good historical analogy would be to the United States government signing a treaty with Mexico giving Mexico a consultative role with respect to both the legal status of, and the domestic affairs in, the North American state of New Mexico. The United States government would never sign such an agreement if it really believed that the legal status and domestic concerns of the state of New Mexico were subject to its exclusive sovereign control.

Moreover, I doubt very seriously that the United States government would ever sign a treaty with Mexico to the effect that if a majority of the people of New Mexico want to join Mexico, then of course the United States Congress would be prepared to pass domestic implementing legislation that cedes New Mexico to Mexico. Quite frankly, I could not envision any set of circumstances under which the United States of America would countenance the return of New Mexico to Mexico. Of course, if American citizens living in New Mexico want to be Mexicans, then they would have the perfect right under international law and the United States Constitution to go to Mexico and expatriate themselves. To be sure, it might also be possible for many individuals who have dual Mexican-American nationalities to live in New Mexico. But even if someday the vast majority of people living in New Mexico were to become dual Mexican-American nationals, I doubt very seriously that the United States Congress would honor any vote by them for the retrocession of New Mexico to Mexico.

Conversely, if the United States government were to sign such a treaty with Mexico over New Mexico, then it would be a pretty good sign that at some particular point in time in the future, the United States would be prepared to countenance the reversion of New Mexico to Mexico. In any event, the conclusion of such a treaty would mean *ipso facto* that both the legal status of, as well as the domestic affairs in, its subject matter (i.e., New Mexico) were matters of international concern and jurisdiction that were no longer subject to the exclusive sovereign control of the United States of America, but henceforth involved Mexico as well as the entire international community, including the United Nations Organization. Today, whatever the legal situation was before 1985, these same principles of international law and world politics now hold true for Northern Ireland.

The Unionists Are Right

I submit that the British government knew full well that it was doing this when it signed the Anglo-Irish Agreement in 1985. In other words, the British government purposely, knowingly, willingly, and voluntarily surrendered its long-standing claim that Northern Ireland was a matter of purely internal concern subject to its exclusive sovereign control alone. I also believe that the British government did this for the express purpose of sending a signal to hard-line Unionists in Northern Ireland of its eventual intention to withdraw from (that is, to decolonize) Northern Ireland.

Thus, I believe that hard-line Unionists in Northern Ireland have performed the appropriate interpretation of the significance of the Anglo-Irish Agreement. This interpretation does not mean that the British government is going to leave Northern Ireland tomorrow. But it seems pretty clear from both the mere existence, as well as the actual contents, of the Anglo-Irish Agreement that the British government will eventually withdraw from Northern Ireland. This interpretation of the Agreement is also consistent with several public statements made by British government officials to the effect that there is no way the Provisional I.R.A. can be defeated militarily.[63]

Hence, the Hillsborough Agreement cannot properly be interpreted as a capitulation by the Irish government to the continued presence of a British colony in Northern Ireland. Even if the FitzGerald government had attempted to do so in 1985, it had no authority to conclude such a treaty that would have expressly violated article 2 of the Irish Constitution: "The national territory consists of the whole island of Ireland, its islands and the territorial seas."[64]* And under international law, the British government was charged with knowledge of this constitutional provision.

---

*Pursuant to the terms of the 1998 Good Friday/Belfast Agreement, the Republic of Ireland amended Articles 2 and 3 of its Constitution in order to render it more palatable to Protestants living in Northern Ireland.

As a party to the Vienna Convention on the Law of Treaties, the British government realized full well that the Irish government had no authority to conclude an international agreement that contradicted Ireland's constitutional claim to Northern Ireland without obtaining a constitutional amendment to that effect, which obviously never occurred.[65] So according to this Vienna Convention provision, the Anglo-Irish Agreement can only be interpreted in a manner consistent with the Irish Constitution and its claim to sovereignty over Northern Ireland. From the perspective of international law, therefore, the Hillsborough Agreement cannot be interpreted as a surrender of the Irish claim to sovereignty over Northern Ireland, but rather, to the contrary, as an implicit British acceptance of that claim.[66]

Conclusion

Commenting upon the reunification of Ireland, the Irish Nobel Peace Prize Winner and former IRA Chief-of-Staff Sean MacBride wrote an *Introduction* to Bobby Sands' autobiography **One Day In My Life** (1983). Robert Sands, M.P., spent the last four and one-half years of his life in the H-Blocks of Long Kesh concentration camp near Belfast. He started a hunger strike on March 8, 1981 in order to protest the Thatcher government's refusal to extend prisoner of war status to captured members of the Irish Republican Army, and eventually died on May 5, 1981.

At the conclusion of his *Introduction*, Sean MacBride wrote approvingly:

> In the early stages of the last decade, Paul Johnson, one of Great Britain's most distinguished journalists, editor of the **Spectator**, and one of Prime Minister Margaret Thatcher's most ardent supporters, wrote in **The New Statesman**:
>
>> In Ireland over the centuries, we have tried every possible formula: direct rule, indirect rule, genocide, apartheid, puppet parliaments, real parliaments, martial law, civil law, colonization, land reform, partition. Nothing has worked. The only solution we have not tried is absolute and unconditional withdrawal. Why not try it now? It will happen in any event!

With public opinion polls consistently demonstrating that only 25% of the British People want to remain in Northern Ireland, this author is fully convinced that he will live to see the termination of British colonial occupation in Northern Ireland and the reunification of the Irish State. It is most tragic and unfortunate that Sean MacBride could not live to see that glorious day for whose realization he had worked an entire lifetime to achieve. But he died fully convinced of inevitable victory for the Irish People.

It is my opinion that over time the vast majority of the British People will manifest their intention to decolonize Northern Ireland. Hence my conclusion that the world community of states should be working now to encourage the British government to publicly adopt the position that it will decolonize Northern Ireland in cooperation with the United Nations Organization and the European Union, and with full and effective guarantees for the Protestants of Northern Ireland under the aforementioned treaties and implementing legislation, as well as under a Bill of Rights incorporated into a new Irish Constitution. Whenever that becomes the official position of the British government, I submit that most of the violence perpetrated by the I.R.A. will terminate, the Irish economy could be reintegrated, and the United States government (together with the E.U.) would then proceed to provide substantial economic assistance to a United Ireland in order to help it get upon its feet.

Pursuant to the proposals outlined above, every person living in a United Ireland—whether Protestant or Catholic, citizen, or resident alien—would have recourse to a domestic court of law and ultimately, to the European Court of Human Rights or the United Nations Human Rights Committee, to assert his or her rights recognized by three seminal international human rights treaties as well as by a constitutionally protected Bill of Rights. Indeed, these substantive and procedural protections would constitute a dramatic step forward toward the progressive liberalization of the human rights situation for the people living in today's Republic of Ireland as well. In other words, under the aforementioned proposals, everyone currently living on the Island of Ireland—whether Protestant or Catholic—would have significantly more substantive and procedural rights in a United Ireland than they possess today in either Northern Ireland or the Republic of Ireland.

In this fashion, a United Ireland could become a "win-win" solution for everyone living there. The concretization of that prospect could provide a substantial incentive for all people currently living on the Island of Ireland to work toward the reunification of the Irish State. There is an enormous amount of work toward progressive reunification that can be done by people of good faith on all sides of this dispute irrespective of the feeble steps toward peace that have been taken by the two governments involved.

The Irish People (whether Protestant or Catholic) living on both sides of this artificial border must no longer allow themselves to remain captives to their respective governments' shortsighted policies. The problems of Northern Ireland have been created and perpetuated by both governments--though, to be sure, to different degrees and in different ways. For the most part, the two governments are the problem, not the solution, to the so-called "troubles" that have plagued Northern Ireland for the past seventy years.

It is time for all the people living on the Island of Ireland to stop looking toward the two governments to produce a solution to the problems of Northern Ireland. Rather, they must look to each other. They must reach out to each other in fraternal solidarity with the full realization that they share more in common with each other than they do with either one of the two governments involved. They must transcend these two governments in order to work toward peaceful reunification on the basis of the "functional-integration" of their inescapably interconnected lives.[67] As the arch-realist himself, Hans Morgenthau, once said: "Thus the future of the civilized world is intimately tied to the functional approach to international organization."[68] The same can be said for the Island of Ireland.[69]

POSTSCRIPT

On 15 December 1993 British Prime Minister John Major and Irish Prime Minister Albert Reynolds concluded the so-called Downing Street Declaration on Northern Ireland. Once again, no point would be served here by analyzing this lengthy document on a line-by-line basis. Suffice it to say that from the perspective of international law and politics, the primary significance of this Declaration was that for the first time ever the British government formally and publicly acknowledged the right of the Irish People to self-determination on the Island of Ireland. The critical passage from the Declaration is as follows:

....

> The British Government agree that it is for the people of the island of Ireland alone, by agreement between the two parts respectively, to exercise their right of self-determination on the basis of consent, freely and concurrently given, north and south, to bring about a united Ireland, if that is their wish.
> They reaffirm as a binding obligation that they will, for their part, introduce the necessary legislation

to give effect to this, or equally to any measure of agreement on future relationships in Ireland which the people living in Ireland may themselves freely so determine without external impediment.

...

To be sure, the Downing Street Declaration built upon the Anglo-Irish Agreement of 1985. Nevertheless, putting aside its ambiguities and obfuscations, the Downing Street Declaration represented a major conceptual breakthrough for the British government: After 800 years of colonial occupation in Ireland, the British government finally recognized the right of the Irish People to self-determination over the Island of Ireland.

Of course, this basic concession on a matter of fundamental principle by the British government was long overdue. But at least and at last it was finally made. This fundamental concession by the British government paved the way for the decision by the Irish Republican Army to announce "a complete cessation of military operations" as of midnight, Wednesday, 31 August 1994. It is hoped that these developments will gradually lead to the creation of a free and United Ireland where Protestants and Catholics can live and work together with peace, harmony, justice, equality, and prosperity for all.

Endnotes

1   *See, e.g.* Francis A. Boyle, *International Law and the Use of Force: Beyond Regime Theory,* in **Ideas and Ideals: Essays on Politics in Honor of Stanley Hoffman** 376-94 (Linda B. Miller and Michael Joseph Smith eds. 1993).

2   *See generally* G. Bell, *The Protestants of Ulster* (1976) 1-4.

3   *See* Walker, *Irish Republican Prisoners – Political Detainees, Prisoners of War or Common Criminals?,* 19 **The Irish Jurist** (1984), 189, 192-193, discussing the British government's policy of criminalizing Irish Republican Army (IRA) paramilitary activity:

> [A] policy of criminalization [. . .] is more likely to maintain or increase public support for the State's counter-measures by emphasizing the criminal and violent aspects of terrorism rather than its political motivation. As a result the public is coaxed into taking a perception of the terrorists which corresponds to that of the State. In other words, the terrorists are viewed simply as criminals, so their treatment as such is acceptable. Depict-

ing the IRA in this light in turn reinforces the official policy of resisting the breaking of the Union. . . . Thus, criminalization is an important conditioning factor to be applied to the minds of the British public, and it is equally aimed at channeling world opinion. Movements denounced as criminal plots rather than freedom fighters are much less likely to receive moral or material support from third States.

See also T. Baldy, **Battle for Ulster** (1987).

4   U.N. Charter Art. 1, para. 2.

5   The International Covenant on Civil and Political Rights, G.A. Res. 2200, 21 U.N. GAOR Supp. (No. 16) at 52, U.N. Doc. A/6316 (1966). The International Covenant on Economic, Social, and Cultural Rights, G.A. Res. 2200, 21 U.N. GAOR Supp. (No. 16) at 49, U.N. Doc A/6316 1966). Part I, Article 1 of both Covenants is identical:

(1) All peoples have the right of self-determination. By virtue of that right they freely determine their political status and freely pursue their economic, social and cultural development.

(2) All peoples may, for their own ends, freely dispose of their natural wealth and resources without prejudice to any obligations arising out of international economic co-operation, based upon the principle of mutual benefit, and international law. In no case may a people be deprived of its own means of subsistence.

(3) The States Parties to the present Covenant, including those having responsibility for the administration of Non-Self-Governing and Trust Territories, shall promote the realization of the right of self-determination, and shall respect that right, in conformity with the provisions of the Charter of the United Nations.

6   *See infra* notes 33-37 and accompanying text. *See also* UNYB (1955), UN Sales No.I956.I.20 pp. 454-55.

7   *See gener*ally F. Boyle, **Defending Civil Resistance Under International Law** 283-316 (1987).

8   The Fourteen Points Address by President Woodrow Wilson, Jan. 8, 1918, *reprinted in* 56 Cong. Rec. 680 (1918). *See* Harvey, *The Right of the People of the Whole of Ireland to Self-Determination, Unity, Sovereignty and Independence,* 11 **N.Y.L. Sch. J. Int'l & Comp. L.** 167(1990).

9   G.A. Res. 1514, 15 U.N. GAOR Supp. (No. 21) at 66, U.N. Doc. A/4684 1960.

10   *Id.* at 67.

11   *Id.*

12   *Id.*

13   *Id.*

14   *Id.*

15   *Id.*

16   G.A. Res. 2625, 25 UN GAOR Supp. No. 28 at 121, UN Doc. A/8082 (1970).

17   *Id.* at 124.

18   *Id.*

19 *Case concerning Military and Paramilitary Activities In and Against Nicaragua* (Nicaragua v. U.S.), 1986 I.C.J. 14 (Judgment of June 27, 1986). The Court stated: "In determining the legal rule which applies to these latter forms, the court can draw on the formulations contained in the Declaration on Principles of International Law concerning Friendly Relations and Co-operation among States in accordance with the Charter of the United Nations (General Assembly resolution 2625 (XXV) referred to above. As already observed, the adoption by the States of this text affords an indication of their *opinio juris* as to customary international law on the question." *Id.* at 101.

20 *See supra* notes 9-19 and accompanying text.

21 *See, e.g.,* **Black's Law Dictionary** 331 (rev. 4th ed. 1968):

"**COLONY.** A dependent political community, consisting of a number of citizens of the same country who have emigrated there from to people another, and remain subject to the mother-country." *U.S. v. The Nancy*, 3 Wash. C.C. 287, Fed. Cas. No. 15,854.

"A settlement in a foreign country possessed and cultivated, either wholly or partially, by immigrants and their descendants, who have a political connection with and subordination to the mother-country, whence they emigrated. In other words, it is a place peopled from some more ancient city or country. Wharton."

Irish Republican groups such as the I.R.A. have justified their opposition to the Union of Northern Ireland with Britain because of the right of the Irish People to self-determination and have called for the end to British colonial occupation. *See* Walker, *supra* note 3, at 189. *See also,* T. Coogan, **The IRA** 685 (3d. ed. 1987). *See generally* J. Bell, **The Irish Troubles** (1993).

22 *See supra* notes 9-15 and accompanying text.

23 Treaty between Great Britain and Ireland, Dec. 6, 1921, 26 L.N.T.S. 9. *See generally* N. Mansergh, **The Unresolved Question** (1991).

24 United Nations Action In the Field of Human Rights at 44, U.N. Doc. ST/HR/2/Rev. 1, U.N. Sales No. E.79.XIV.6 (1980). *See* B. Urquhart, **Decolonization and World Peace** (1989).

25 24 U.N. SCOR Supp. (July-Sep. 1969) at 159, U.N. Doc. S/9394 (1969).

26 24 U.N. SCOR Res. & Dec. at 8, U.N. Doc. S/INF/24/Rev. 1 (1969).

27 1969 U.N.Y.B. 181, U.N. Sales No. E.71.I1.

28 24 U.N. GAOR (180th mtg.) at 4, U.N. Doc. A/BUR/SR 180 (1969).

29 *See* 7 **U.N. Monthly Chron.** 69 (1970), where Irish Prime Minister John M. Lynch stated to the General Assembly: "Ireland has suffered much from war, and in the past two years there have been serious difficulties in the North of Ireland. Britain retained responsibility for that small part of Ireland when it retired from the rest. We believe that community will see that its future lies with Ireland." *See also* 8 **U.N. Monthly Chron.** 165-6 (1971); 9 **U.N. Monthly Chron.** 106 (1977); 15 **U.N. Monthly Chron.** 93 (1978).

30   U.N. Charter art. 24, para. 1 states: "In order to ensure prompt and ef-
         fective action by the United Nations, its members confer on the Security
         Council primary responsibility for the maintenance of international
         peace and security, and agree that in carrying out its duties under this
         responsibility the Security Council acts on their behalf."

31   I. Rikhye, M. Harbottle, & B. Eyge, **The Thin Blue Line: International
         Peacekeeping And Its Future** 3 (1974). *See, e.g.,* Myers, *A New Rem-
         edy for Northern Ireland: The Case for United Nations Peacekeeping
         Intervention in an Internal Conflict,* 11 **N.Y.L. Sch. J. Int'l & Comp. L.** 1
         (1990).

32   D. Doumitt, **Conflict In Northern Ireland** 189 (1985). A number of so-
         lutions to the problem in Northern Ireland have been suggested. For
         example, Dr. Garret FitzGerald, former leader of the Fine Gael Party in
         the Republic suggested making Northern Ireland and the Republic a
         confederation. *Id. See also* **Report of the New Ireland Forum** (2 May
         1984).

33   *See supra* notes 5-6 and accompanying text.

34   1977 Gr. Brit. T.S. No. 6 (Cmd. 6702).

35   *See* Power & Quinn, *Ireland's Accession to the United Nations' Human
         Rights Covenants,* 7 **Ir. L.T.R.** 36 (1989).

36   G.A. Res. 2200, 21 U.N. GAOR Supp. (No. l16) at 59, U.N. Doc. A16316
         (1966).

37   European Convention for the Protection of Human Rights and
         Fundamental Freedoms, Nov. 4, 1950, 213 U.N.T.S. 221. The Convention
         was drafted by the member states of the Council of Europe and was
         opened for ratification on Nov. 4, 1950. The Convention entered into
         force in September of 1953 after the deposit of ten instruments of
         ratification with the Secretary General of the Council of Europe. *Id.* at
         222.

38   Ireland has not adopted domestic implementing legislation for any one
         of these three treaties. Under Irish domestic law, following the British
         model, treaties are not deemed to be self-executing, and therefore can-
         not be relied upon to state a cause of action in domestic court without
         domestic implementation by Parliament. *McGimpsey v. Ireland,* 1988
         I.R. 567, 581.

39   In 2003 the Parliament of the Republic of Ireland passed the European
         Convention on Human Rights Act, which partially incorporated into
         domestic law the European Convention on Human Rights and several
         of its Protocols that the State had ratified since 1953.

40   *See generally* Amnesty International, **Human Rights Concerns in the
         United Kingdom** 56-60 (June 1991); Bishop, *The Right To Be Arrested,* 11
         N.Y. L. Sch. J. Int'l & Comp. L., 207, 208-11 (1990); Note, *Terrorists and
         Special Status: The British Experience in Northern Ireland,* 9 **Hastings
         Int'l & Comp. L. Rev.** 481, 500 (1986). Furthermore, throughout the
         history of Northern Ireland, Britain has enacted special legislation to
         deal with so-called "terrorist activity" there. The first was the Civil
         Authorities(Special Powers) Acts of 1922-23, 12 & 13 Geo. 5, ch. 5.

These were replaced with the Northern Ireland (Emergency Provisions) Act, 1973, ch. 53, *reprinted in* 43 Halsbury's Statutes of England 1235 (3d ed. 1970). This was re-enacted without significant changes in 1978. It was also amended in 1987.

41 According to British law, treaties are not deemed to be self-executing. *See* McNair, **The Law of Treaties** 81 (1961), stating: "In the United Kingdom, as we shall see, with a very limited class of exception, no treaty is self-executing; no treaty requiring municipal action to give effect to it can receive that effect without the cooperation of Parliament, either in the form of a statute or in some other way." The British government has not ratified the Optional Protocol to the ICCPR. Levin & Edwards, *The UK Human Rights Network*, in **Human Rights in the United Kingdom** 138 (1988). It has not incorporated the Council of Europe's Convention for the Protection of Human Rights and Fundamental Freedoms, Boyle, *Freedom of Expression*, *id.* at 86; and neither has it incorporated the European Convention on Human Rights. Shaw, *Prisoner's Rights*, *id.* at 41. And the ICCPR has not been made part of U.K. domestic law. *R. v. Secretary of State for the Home Department, ex parte Weeks*, Q.B. (Crown Office List) CO/1338/87 (1988).

42 *See* Doumitt, *supra* note 32, at 71-94.

43 *Id. See also* Abramovsky, *The Political Offense Exception and the Extradition Process: The Enhancement of the Role of the U.S. Judiciary,* 13 **Hastings Int'l & Comp. L. Rev.** 1, 3 (1989). One of the most infamous events in Northern Ireland's history was "bloody Sunday" when British armed forces in Londonderry killed thirteen Catholic demonstrators engaged in peaceful civil resistance activities on Jan. 30, 1972. *Id.*

44 *See* Bell, *supra* note 2, at 1. *See also* Doumitt, *supra* note 32, at 152-57.

45 *Accord* The Norwegian Helsinki Committee, **Irish Terrorism or British Colonialism? The Violation of Human Rights in Northern Ireland** (July 1990). *See also* Amnesty International, **United Kingdom: Political Killings in Northern Ireland** (February, 1994). Indeed the I.R.A. has always claimed to be waging a war of national liberation on behalf of the Irish People against alien (British) rule. Connelly, *Political Violence and International Law: The Case of Northern Ireland*, 16 **Den. J. Int'l L. & Pol'y** 79 (1987). *See generally* T. Coogan, **The IRA: A History** (1993).

46 J. Hatch, **The History of Britain In Africa** 197 (1969). *See also*, Doumitt, *supra* note 32, at 208, stating: "The practice of dividing the conquered was a long established method of British rule."

47 *Id.*

48 *See* K. Boyle, T. Hadden, & P. Hillyard, **Law And State -- The Case of Northern Ireland** 29-36 (1975). *See also* Doumitt, *supra* note 32, at 152-163.

49 Treaty Establishing the European Economic Community, March 25, 1957, 298 U.N.T.S. 11 (entered into force Jan. 1, 1958). The original signatories were Belgium, France, Germany, Italy, Luxembourg and the Netherlands. *Id.* Denmark, Ireland, and the United Kingdom be-

came members on Jan. 1, 1973. *See* Toepke, *The European Economic Community—A Profile.* 3 **Nw. J. Int'l L. & Bus.** 640, 643 (1981).

50 *See* Walker, *supra* note 3, at 190, stating: "In reply to Republican apologists the official line likewise calls in the internationally hallowed principle of self-determination but this time on behalf of the separatist Loyalist 'people.'" *See also Cooper, Humanitarian Intervention: A Possibility for Northern Ireland*, 12 **Den. J. Int'l L. & Pol'y.** 297, 298 (1983), stating:

> The British Government also justifies its actions as a means of fulfilling a formal promise not to abandon Northern Ireland's one million Protestants. The pledge, "the guarantee," as it is called, is a section of the 1973 Constitution Act, which reads: "It is hearby affirmed that in no way will Northern Ireland or any part of it cease to be part of Her Majesty's dominion and of the United Kingdom without the consent of the majority of people in Northern Ireland, voting in a poll."

51 At its height during the late 19th and early 20th centuries, the British empire comprised about one quarter of the world's area and population. Over 600 million people were ruled from London. 4 **Oxford Illustrated Encyclopaedia World History From 1800 to the Present Day** 51 (1988). *See also* 19 **The New Encyclopaedia Britannica** 521 (15th ed. 1988); **The Times Atlas of World History, European Colonial Empires** 1815-1914, at 244-55 (1979).

52 Hong Kong's population at the time the treaty was signed was 5.5 million. *See* N.Y. Times, Sept. 27, 1984, at 1, col. 3. Draft Agreement Between the United Kingdom of Great Britain and Northern Ireland, and the Government of the People's Republic of China on the Future of Hong Kong, White Paper (Sept. 26, 1984), *reprinted in* 23 I.L.M. 1366 (1984). *See also* Mushkat, *The Transition from British to Chinese Rule in Hong Kong--A Discussion of Salient International Legal Issues*, 14 **Den. J. Int'l L. & Pol'y** 171 (1986).

53 *See* Doumitt, *supra* note 32, at 222.

54 Agreement between the Government of the United Kingdom and the Government of Ireland, *signed* Nov. 15, 1985, *reprinted in* 24 I.L.M. 1582 (1985). The agreement was subject to ratification and was to enter into force on the date on which the two governments exchanged notifications of their acceptance. The Irish Parliament approved the agreement on Nov. 21, 1985 and the British Parliament approved it on Nov. 27, 1985. Notifications of acceptance were exchanged on Nov. 29, 1985. *See* 24 I.L.M. 1579 (1985).

55 UN Charter Art. 2, para. 7, stating: "Nothing contained in the present Charter shall authorize the United Nations to intervene in matters which are essentially within the domestic jurisdiction of any state or shall require the members to submit such matters to settlement under the present Charter; but this principle shall not prejudice the application of enforcement measures under Chapter VII."

56   *See* 19 **The New Encyclopaedia Britannica** 521 (15th ed. 1988).

57   *See supra* note 54 and accompanying text.

58   *See* Anglo-Irish Treaty, *supra* note 54, at 1583-84. The treaty gives Ireland a formal role in governing Northern Ireland for the first time since Ireland's partition in 1921.

59   *See also* Note, *Bridging The Irish Sea: The Anglo-Irish Treaty of 1985*, 12 **Syr. J. Int'l L. & Com.** 585, 588 (1986).

60   Nationality Decrees In Tunis and Morocco, 1923 P.C.I.J. (ser. E) No. 1, at 195 (Feb. 7).

61   U.N. Charter art. 102 states: "Every treaty and every international agreement entered into by any Member of the United Nations after the present Charter comes into force shall as soon as possible be registered with the Secretariat and published by it."

62   *See supra* note 54, at 1583.

63   *See* Coogan, *supra* note 21, at 472. *See also* M. Farrell, **Northern Ireland: The Orange State** 332 (1976).

64   The Republic of Ireland Constitution Art. II. In this regard, Article 3 further provides: "Pending the re-integration of the national territory, and without prejudice to the right of the Parliament and Government established by this Constitution to exercise jurisdiction over the whole of that territory, the laws enacted by that Parliament shall have the like area and extent of application as the laws of Sarorstat Eireann and the like extra-territorial effect."

65   Vienna Convention on the Law of Treaties, May 23, 1969, 1155 U.N.T.S. 331 (came into force Jan. 27, 1980). Article 46 thereof provides as follows:

   PART V. INVALIDITY, TERMINATION AND SUSPENSION OF THE OPERATION OF TREATIES
   SECTION 1. GENERAL PROVISIONS

   . . . .

   SECTION 2. INVALIDITY OF TREATIES
   Article 46. Provisions of Internal Law
   Regarding Competence to Conclude Treaties
   1) A State may not invoke the fact that its consent to be bound by a treaty has been expressed in violation of a provision of its internal law regarding competence to conclude treaties as invalidating its consent unless that violation was manifest and concerned a rule of its internal law of fundamental importance.
   (2) A violation is manifest if it would be objectively evident to any State conducting itself in the matter in accordance with normal practice and in good faith.

   See also I. Sinclair, **The Vienna Convention On The Law Of Treaties** 159-97 (2d. ed. 1984).

66   *But compare* A. Coughlan, **Fooled Again?** (1986).

67   *See, e.g.,* D. Mitrany, **The Functional Theory of Politics** (1975).

68   *See* Morgenthau, *Introduction* to D. Mitrany, **A Working Peace System** 7, at 11 (1966).

69   *See, e.g.,* House, *The Border That Wouldn't Go Away: Irish Integration in the EC,* 11 **N.Y. L. Sch. J. Int'l & Comp. L.** 229 (1990).

CHAPTER THREE

PUTTING BRITAIN'S COLONIAL WAR IN IRELAND ON TRIAL IN THE USA

It is always a nice little academic exercise for some professor to write and publish a scholarly article that analyzes with clinical detachment a highly complicated and extremely emotional mixed-dispute involving international law and international politics along the lines of the previous chapter. It is quite another thing for that professor then to go into a United States Federal District Court on behalf of a defendant being prosecuted by the United States government for alleged involvement in "international terrorism" and present that scholarly argument under oath and subject to cross-examination by an Assistant United States Attorney under the auspices of a hostile United Stated Federal District Judge. The courtroom has always proved to be the "acid test" for any professor's scholarly opinion. If the professor can withstand withering cross-examination by the U.S. government's attorney and repeated hostile interruptions and questioning by the U.S. government's judge, then that is a pretty good indication that he must know what he is talking about and, most importantly, that what he has to say is true. After all, the adversarial nature of U.S. courtroom proceedings is specifically designed to bring to light the truth so that justice might be administered on the basis of truth. At least that is the theory of justice here in America.

This chapter sets forth a blow-by-blow account of what happened in a United States Federal District Court when we put on trial Britain's colonial war in Ireland in order to defend a group of Irish citizens from prosecution by the United States government for allegedly trying to purchase military weapons—including and especially a Stinger missile—that were allegedly intended to be used by the Irish Republican Army to shoot down British military helicopters in Northern Ireland at one of the most intense moments in the conflict over there. The reader should get an excellent idea of what happened in Federal Court when I presented the arguments set forth in Chapter 2 on behalf of their Defense. You are free to draw your own conclusions about the validity of what I had to say. But this slightly edited courtroom transcript certainly makes for compelling reading.

Britain's colonial occupation Army had established military outposts right near the non-demarcated "border" between Northern Ireland and the Republic of Ireland that I had already tried to tour myself in 1986. The I.R.A. had been so successful in its military operations in these "border" areas that it had cut off the capability of the British Army to supply those outposts by ground transportation. So Britain had to supply these Army outposts by military helicopters. At all times relevant to these proceedings, American Stinger missiles were proving their deadly efficacy in Afghanistan where the United States government had provided them to the Mujahideen in order to shoot down the Soviet Union's military helicopters prosecuting their criminal invasion, occupation, and war against Afghanistan and its People.

In this case, the basic theory of the Defense was that like the Soviet Union in Afghanistan, **Britain was fighting an illegal anti-colonial war in Northern Ireland and therefore that the I.R.A. had the perfect right to use military force in self-defense against military targets**, including and especially by employing Stinger missiles. This Defense was built upon the theoretical analysis set forth in my then draft working paper, The Decolonization of Northern Ireland, set forth in Chapter 2 above. Throughout this entire prosecution the United States government was working at all times in full cooperation with the British government—"our great and noble ally."

The Federal District Judge was extremely hostile to the Defense and did everything possible to shut it down. Furthermore, while the proceedings were taking place, the I.R.A. was conducting major military operations against Britain that exerted a highly deleterious impact on these legal proceedings here in the United States.[1] Heavy-duty security measures were imposed at the courthouse that were specifically intended by the U.S. government to exert a negative emotional impact upon the jury. Yet, it was well-known that as a matter of policy the I.R.A. did not launch military operations anywhere near, in, or upon the United States of America, whose Irish American population was its greatest source of foreign support.

Ultimately, the defendants were convicted on (1) one count of conspiracy for trying to obtain a military weapon; and (2) one count of conspiracy for attempting to obtain an explosive that crossed state lines with the intent to destroy people or property. But they were acquitted on counts charging them with (1) attempting to transport an explosive in foreign commerce; (2) attempting to export defense weapons without a license; and (3) violating the United States Neutrality Act.[2] This was an outstanding result that basically vindicated our theory of the Defense. Most notably, the acquittal on the last count was a major victory for the Defense because we had from the very outset of the case taken the position that the U.S. Neutrality Act did not apply to protect Britain with respect to its waging an anti-colonial war in Ireland.[3]

At the end of the proceedings the defendants were each sentenced to four years in prison.[4] A remarkable result for parties stashing a live Stinger missile in the boot of a car and driving up Florida's A1A Highway! And a great tribute to the outstanding caliber of the Defense team of lawyers (including the late, great Frank Durkan: R.I.P.); to the power of the international law arguments; to the common sense of the jury; and to the basic fair-mindedness of the new sentencing judge who had replaced the hostile trial judge at the request of the Defense for good cause. Now if that sentencing judge had been the original trial judge we might have gotten them all off scot-free!

This prosecution and result demonstrates the complete and total hypocrisy of the United States government when it comes to the phenomenon known as "international terrorism." The United States government itself was providing Stinger missiles to freedom fighters in Afghanistan (some of whom later became Al Qaeda) to be used against the Soviet Union that had illegally invaded and occupied that country, while at the exact same time prosecuting Irish nationals for trying to provide the exact same American Stinger missiles to freedom fighters in Ireland to be used against the illegal, colonial, military invasion and occupation of their country by Britain.

UNITED STATES DISTRICT COURT
SOUTHERN DISTRICT OF FLORIDA
MIAMI DIVISION

UNITED STATES OF AMERICA

Plaintiff

-vs-

KEVIN MCKINLEY,
SEMUS MOLE,
JOSEPH McCOLGAN,

Defendants.

Case No. 90-8005-Cr-JAG

December 4, 1989
Ft. Lauderdale, Florida

TRANSCRIPT OF TESTIMONY OF
PROFESSOR FRANCIS A. BOYLE
BEFORE THE HONORABLE JOSE A. GONZALEZ

APPEARANCES:

For the Government:

FRANK TAMEN, Assistant
United States Attorney
155 South Miami Avenue
Miami, Florida 33130

For the Defendant McKinley:

FRED HADDAD, Esquire

For Defendant Moley:

BRUCE ZIMET, Esquire

For Defendant McColgan:

STEPHEN BRONIS and
FRANK DURKAN, Esquires

Court Reporter:

Barbara Medina
301 North Miami Avenue
Miami, Florida 33128

(Call to order of the Court.)

*　　　　　*　　　　　*　　　　　*

THE DEPUTY CLERK: Please raise your right hand.

PROFESSOR FRANCIS A. BOYLE,
DEFENDANT McCOLGAN'S WITNESS SWORN

THE DEPUTY CLERK: Please be seated.

Would you, please, state your name and spell your last name for the record?
THE WITNESS: My name is Francis A. Boyle, B-o-y-l-e.
DIRECT EXAMINATION
BY MR. BRONIS:
Q   How are you employed, sir?
A   I am a professor of international law at the University of Illinois College of Law in Champaign, Illinois.
. . . .
Q   Have you testified in court and been qualified as an expert in court in the area of international law?
A   Yes, I have.
Q   Professor Boyle, do you agree with the proposition that the conflict in Northern Ireland is an internal sectarian conflict?
A   No, I do not.
Q   Is the conflict in Northern Ireland an entirely internal conflict at all?
A   No. Under basic principles of international law, what you have in Northern Ireland is a case of colonial –
MR. TAMEN: I object to the relevance of this.
THE COURT: Overruled.
A   What you have is a case of colonial occupation, similar to many different types of colonial occupations that we have seen around the world in various portions of the world by former colonial imperial powers such as Britain or France.

Under the relevant principles of international law, Britain is under an absolute obligation to withdraw from Northern Ireland.

MR. TAMEN: I have an objection here.

THE COURT: Sustained. What is the relevance of all this, Mr. Bronis?

MR. BRONIS: If I can ask my next question?

THE COURT: Let me hear it.

BY MR. BRONIS:

Q   Under international law, what right, if any, does the Irish Republican Army have to use force or the threat of force directed against British military property?

THE COURT: That's irrelevant.

MR. BRONIS: May we have a sidebar?

THE COURT: No, sir.

BY MR. BRONIS:

Q   Under international law would the Irish Republican Army have the right to use a Stinger missile against a British Army helicopter situated in Northern Ireland?

MR. TAMEN: I am going to object.

THE COURT: That's irrelevant.

MR. TAMEN: I would like to have a standing objection as to any questions as to what international law is.

THE COURT: You may have that.

This is a United States Court, not an international law court.

MR. BRONIS: Your Honor, I would like to proffer what the witness's answer will be.

THE COURT: You may proffer them after the jury has been excused.

BY MR. BRONIS:

Q   Would the use by the Irish Republican Army of a Stinger missile against a British Army helicopter be considered terrorism or an act of terrorism?

THE COURT: That's irrelevant.

MR. BRONIS: Your Honor, the Government has—

THE COURT: That's irrelevant.

BY MR. BRONIS:

Q   Is the British Army entitled to transport women and children in military helicopters?

A   No.

MR. TAMEN: Objection, Your Honor, to the relevance and foundation for this opinion.

THE COURT: Overruled.

A   Under basic principles of international law, when you are in a situation of international armed conflict such as the case in Northern

Ireland, military forces are obliged to refrain from involving civilians directly in the conflict.

At best, the British Army, if there is a need to transport civilians, should be using civilian helicopters with the Red Cross of the Geneva Convention clearly affixed on the helicopter itself.

They should not be using military helicopters to transport civilians.

Q   Is your description of the war in Northern Ireland as an anti-colonial war, is that analogous to any other current international conflict, if any?

MR. TAMEN: Objection. Relevance.

THE COURT: Sustained.

MR. BRONIS: I have no further questions.

. . . .

THE COURT: Mr. Tamen.

CROSS EXAMINATION
BY MR. TAMEN:

Q   The British Government obviously disagrees with your opinion on whether or not they can use their helicopters to transport civilians.

Would that be a fair statement?

A   That's not binding under international law, what their opinion is. I am here testifying as an expert to the requirements of international law, not what the British Government may or may not think about it.

Q   My question was the British Government obviously has a different opinion than you as to whether or not they can legally use their helicopters to transport civilians.

Would that be a fair statement?

A   Well, the British Government has recently changed its position on the character of the status of the conflict in Northern Ireland. By signing the Anglo-Irish Agreement, they have elevated the situation in Northern Ireland to an international conflict over internationally disputed territory.

Their position had been before this Agreement that the conflict in Northern Ireland was purely internal concerns, subject to their laws alone. After the Anglo-Irish Accord of 1985, that's no longer the case.

So I am not exactly sure precisely what their international legal position would be today.

Q   But as a matter of policy, they do it?

A   Do what, counsel?

Q   Transport civilians in military helicopters?

A   I don't know if they do or they don't.

Q   Okay.

A   As I said before, if they do, they should not be using military helicopters to transport civilians.

Q   If there was some natural disaster like a flood or something like that, it would be improper for them to use military helicopters to evacuate civilians from danger?

A   In an international armed conflict of this nature, the requirements of the Geneva Convention are quite clear. They must clearly affix the symbol of the Red Cross to the helicopter.

If they have the symbol of the Red Cross clearly affixed, then it would be acceptable.

Q   Suppose they haven't got time to do that because of danger to life, then what would your position be?

A   They should use a civilian helicopter.

Q   If they haven't got one?

A   I take it they do have these helicopters.

Again, the rules are quite clear, in a combat zone, you are not to be transporting civilians with a military helicopter for any reason.

MR. TAMEN: I have no further questions.

REDIRECT EXAMINATION
BY MR. BRONIS:

Q   Are the rules before international law, as you have stated them for Mr. Tamen, are those international law rules by which all civilized countries are to conduct themselves?

MR. TAMEN: I am going to have to object.

A   That's correct.

THE COURT: Do you have any reason to believe the United Kingdom does not possess civilian helicopters?

THE WITNESS: No. I understand they have a fairly large number of helicopters.

BY MR. BRONIS:

Q   Have you heard of any situation where the United Kingdom has professed to run out of Red Cross symbols?

A   No.

MR. BRONIS: I have no further questions.

THE COURT: Step down, Mr. Boyle. Next witness, please.

THE WITNESS: Thank you.

MR. BRONIS: Your Honor, if Professor Boyle can stay? I did want to be able to proffer—

THE COURT: Yes, sir. Have a seat in the courtroom, if you can find a place.

. . . .

THE COURT: Be seated please. Come to order. Mr. Bronis, you wanted to proffer some evidence.

MR. BRONIS: Yes, if Professor Boyle could take the stand.

THE COURT: All right. Professor Boyle, would you take the stand again, please?

You were sworn earlier. You are reminded you are still under oath.

Let the record reflect we are now proceeding on an offer of proof on behalf of the defense.

DIRECT EXAMINATION
BY MR. BRONIS:

Q Professor Boyle, under international law, having described the conflict in Northern Ireland as an anti-colonial war and an international armed conflict, under international law what right, if any, does the Irish Republican Army have to use force or the threat of force?

A Groups such as the I.R.A. fighting anti-colonial wars have the right to use military force in order to terminate a clearly illegal colonial occupation as is the case in Northern Ireland.

Q Under international law, does that recognized right or privilege to use force include the right to use a Stinger missile directed against a British Army helicopter situated in Northern Ireland?

A As long as the target of the military force is military and not civilian.

That answer to that question is yes.

Q Would the use by the Irish Republican Army of a Stinger missile against a British Army helicopter be considered terrorism or an act of terrorism under international law?

A No. Under international law, it would be an act of war.

Q What, if any, current international conflicts are analogous to the use of a Stinger missile by the I.R.A. against a British Army helicopter in Northern Ireland?

A The situation in Afghanistan where the United States Government has provided Stinger missiles to guerilla fighters in Afghanistan to shoot down Soviet helicopters—it's precisely analogous as far as international law is concerned.

MR. BRONIS: Your Honor that's all—

THE COURT: How do you know the U.S. Government has provided missiles to people in Afghanistan?

THE WITNESS: Your Honor, I think that is a matter of public record.

THE COURT: Where?

THE WITNESS: As an expert I have read quite extensively in books, newspaper articles, magazines, Congressional hearings, and things of this nature.

THE COURT: Oh, so what you are telling me is hearsay?

THE WITNESS: No, Your Honor. I believe that this is a matter that experts in my field do rely upon.

The only people who would have better information—

THE COURT: What you are telling me is an exception to hearsay?

THE WITNES: Well, Your Honor, the only people who might have better information than I are those in the Central Intelligence Agency who directly supply the Stinger missiles.

And I take it they would not be allowed to testify in this Court here today.

But generally, experts in my field who do study this, do rely on a high degree of information that has come into the public records.

THE COURT: Okay. Did you wish to cross examine the proffer, Mr. Haddad.

MR. HADDAD: No, sir.

. . . .

Endnotes

1   *See, e.g.,* Alexander MacLeod, *IRA Attacks Prod Thatcher,* Christian Science Monitor, Sept. 24, 1990.

2   *Verdicts Against 3 Irishmen,* Palm Beach Post, Dec. 12, 1990, at 1; Jodi Mailander, *Missile Customers Convicted, id.*

3   Here the Defense relied upon the historical analysis of the U.S. Neutrality Act that was later published in my **Foundations of World Order** 127-31 (1999).

4   *3 IRA Men Sentenced,* Newsday, June 9, 1991, at 16.

CHAPTER FOUR

THE STRUGGLE TO FREE JOE DOHERTY

The previous chapters established that the Irish Republican Army and its splinter groups constitute the National Liberation Movement of the Irish People under international law and in particular according to Article 1 paragraph 4 of Additional Protocol I to the Four Geneva Conventions of 1949:

> *The situations referred to in the preceding paragraph include armed conflicts in which peoples are fighting against colonial domination and alien occupation and against racist régimes in the exercise of their right of self-determination, as enshrined in the Charter of the United Nations and the Declaration on Principles of International Law concerning Friendly Relations and Co-operation among States in accordance with the Charter of the United Nations.*

Britain officially acknowledged the right to self-determination of the Irish People living on the entire Island of Ireland by means of the 15 December 1993 Downing Street Declaration on Northern Ireland and subsequent agreements.[1] All of Ireland is their self-determination unit. Britain is also a separate self-determination unit. Northern Ireland is part of the Irish self-determination unit. Thus, Northern Ireland is not a separate self-determination unit.

Furthermore, historically the Irish People have been "fighting against colonial domination and alien occupation and against racist régimes" that Britain has established and maintained in Ireland for centuries. When it comes to Ireland, Britain imposed "colonial domination" and "alien occupation" and "racist régimes" against the Irish People that continue as of today in six Irish counties in the Northeast of Ireland. Indeed, Ireland has been and still is Britain's first and longest-standing colony.

Accordingly, IRA Volunteers were soldiers fighting in an international armed conflict against Britain in accordance with and subject to the Laws of War and as well as International Humanitarian Law, which includes Additional Protocol I and the Four Geneva Conventions of 1949 and Article 4(a)(3) of the Third Convention of 1949 Relative to the Treatment of Prisoners of War. The practical consequences of this conclusion were dramatically demonstrated by the case of the most celebrated IRA Volunteer in the annals of American Jurisprudence: Joseph Doherty.

When former IRA Chief-of-Staff and Irish Nobel Peace Prize Laureate Sean MacBride personally asked me to work on Joe's case, I immediately called up his superlative attorneys, Mary Pike and Steve Somerstein, and volunteered my professional services free of charge.

To make a very long story short because it will be explained in more detail in the documents below: In 1980 Joe was an IRA Volunteer who was engaged in a fire-fight on the streets of Northern Ireland—the land of his birth—by a unit of colonial Britain's Special Air Service (SAS) that had laid an ambush for him and his IRA comrades. The SAS was a key component of British occupation forces, and had always operated as a British death squad with shoot-to-kill orders against IRA Volunteers. Their presence in Northern Ireland could not be understood in any other way than as a force intended not merely to maintain the occupation, but to actively search out and kill elements of the Irish resistance seeking to liberate their homeland from colonial, alien invaders—effectively acts of war within Northern Ireland. When Joe killed an SAS captain before Britain's SAS assassin killed Joe, he did so while on his homeland, in the context of an intended SAS targeting and engagement, and as part of an ongoing international armed conflict.

Apprehended and put on trial before Britain's kangaroo court system in Northern Ireland better known under the moniker of the Diplock Courts, Joe and some fellow IRA Volunteers then organized a daring escape from jail. Joe made his way to the United States—"the land of the free and the home of the brave"—where he lived and worked inconspicuously as a bartender in New York City until arrested by the FBI in 1983. Back home Joe had been convicted in absentia of "murdering" the SAS assassin and sentenced to life in prison.

Joe was then imprisoned in the Metropolitan Correctional Center in Manhattan where I visited with him. Working hand-in-glove with the Anglophile Reagan administration and then the Anglophile Bush Sr. administration, Britain proceeded to subject Joe to nine years of *protracted legal proceedings in order to extradite him for a crime back to Northern Ireland. When that failed, Britain sought to have him deported back home for having illegally entered the United States. After losing in the United States Supreme Court on that issue, Joe was deported—not extradited for a crime—back to jail in Northern Ireland in 1992, and then transferred to the Maze Prison for IRA Volunteers. Under the terms of the Good Friday/Belfast Peace Agreement, Joe was released from prison and promptly became a community worker trying to produce peace and reconciliation in Northern Ireland.[2]*

The following documents relate to my efforts to free Joe Doherty here in the United States and prevent his deportation back to Britain. They explain the legal and human rights issues at stake for Joe and other IRA Volunteers in such a situation. First comes a Keynote Address I delivered on Joe's behalf at a rally held by Chicago's Irish American Community at U.S. Federal Plaza in Downtown Chicago on June 17, 1989.

While all this was going on, I was elected to serve two two-year terms on the Board of Directors of Amnesty International USA from 1988 to 1992 by its membership. So next comes my December 3, 1990 Memorandum in my capacity as an AIUSA Board member addressed to two of my fellow AIUSA Board members requesting the formal intervention by Amnesty International headquartered in London and by Amnesty International USA headquartered in New York City. Pursuant to my request, and to their great credit, both Amnesty International and Amnesty International USA thrice intervened on Joe's behalf. Also reprinted below is a 4 April 1991 letter by the Deputy Secretary General of Amnesty International in London to U.S. Attorney General Richard Thornburgh in support of Joe's request to reopen his asylum claim. Then on January 31, 1992 Jack Healey, Executive Director of Amnesty International USA— my good friend and fellow Irish American—wrote to U.S. Attorney General William P. Barr after Joe had lost in the U.S. Supreme Court requesting that Barr reopen Joe's case and permit a hearing on his claims for asylum and withholding of deportation. In addition, both Amnesty International and Amnesty International USA submitted a Brief amici curiae on behalf of Joe into the United States Supreme Court. They were specially bound in Green covers—a nice political touch that was greatly appreciated by all concerned.[3] These three separate interventions by Amnesty International and Amnesty International USA on behalf of Joe speak for themselves.

Taken together these three AI and AI/AIUSA interventions attest to the fact that by acquiescing to pressure from the British government, the Reagan administration, and the Bush Sr. administration deprived Joe of his basic human rights and his rights under the United States Constitution, Statutes, and under Treaties to which the United States government is a contracting party, reflecting a political vendetta waged by the British government with the full cooperation of the Anglophile Republican Party Establishment during both U.S. administrations.

"No more Joe Dohertys!" That was the slogan we Irish Americans rallied around in order to help defeat Bush Sr. in his presidential re-election campaign for 1992. Irish Americans also knocked off Dick Thornburgh when he ran to be elected U.S. Senator from Pennsylvania in 1991. It was payback for Joe. American politicians thwart Irish America at their peril!

There is a saying to the effect that the Irish "never forgive and never forget." Whether or not that proposition is true for the Irish, it certainly holds true for Perfidious Albion. While the deportation of Joe Doherty was not prevented, a mobilized Irish America succeeded in effectively gutting Margaret Thatcher's 1985 U.S.-U.K. Supplementary Extradition Treaty, forcing Britain to walk away and lick its wounds.

But Britain never surrendered its plans to fight its interminable anti-Irish war at a more propitious time. Sadly, exploiting the terrible tragedy of September 11, 2001, the British Empire soon thereafter struck back at Irish America with an even more totalitarian Extradition Treaty. That will be the subject of the next chapter in this book—and Irish America's so far successful defense against its inveterate enemy.

FREE JOE DOHERTY—IRELAND'S PATRIOT, AMERICA'S PRISONER
June 17, 1989

It would only be appropriate for us to start these proceedings by quoting from Illinois' favorite son, Abraham Lincoln, the great liberator himself. On January 12, 1848, Lincoln gave an address to the United States House of Representatives on the peoples' right to Revolution:

> Any people anywhere, being inclined and having the power, have the *right* to rise up, and shake off the existing government, and form a new one that suits them better. This is a most valuable—a most sacred right—a right, which we hope and believe, is to liberate the world. Nor is this right confined to cases in which the whole people of an existing government may choose to exercise it. Any portion of such people that *can, may* revolutionize, and make their *own*, of so much of the territory [*sic*] as they inhabit. . . . I. Basler, The Collected Works of Abraham Lincoln 438-439 (1953).

That was Abraham Lincoln before the United States House of Representatives on January 12, 1848. Lincoln's exact same principles should also apply to Joe Doherty on June 17, 1989 in New York City. Yet today, Joe begins his seventh year of illegal incarceration in Manhattan's Metropolitan Correctional Center.

Joe Doherty engaged in armed combat with an SAS squad on the streets of northern Ireland. As you know, the SAS is no better than an organized assassination team that carries out Margaret Thatcher's shoot-to-kill policy in Northern and now Gibraltar. During the course of this armed combat, Joe fought and killed a British soldier before he killed Joe. Unlike that British soldier, however, Joe was fighting for the freedom and independence of his own homeland.

In this regard, Joe was just like George Washington, Thomas Jefferson, Alexander Hamilton, and the other Founding Fathers of the United States of America. They too fought and killed British soldiers in order to obtain independence and freedom for their homeland, which we are privileged to inhabit today. Just as now we here in the United States of America revere Washington, Jefferson, and Hamilton as American patriots and heroes, someday the Irish people will revere Joe Doherty as an Irish patriot and hero.

Joe was captured by the British and eventually convicted before a rump tribunal without any basic protections of due process of law. He escaped from prison, and shortly thereafter Thatcher made a vow in the House of Parliament that Joe would be returned. Thatcher was prepared to hunt Joe down to the very ends of the earth, just as she hunted down and murdered Mairead Farrell and her two colleagues in Gibraltar.

For his own protection, Joe fled to the United States of America—land of the free and home of the brave—that is, the home of Washington, Hamilton, and Jefferson. Joe sought refuge among those whose Founding Fathers had fought and killed British soldiers in order to obtain their independence and freedom from British oppression and colonial rule over 200 years ago. Surely among all the nations in the world, the one country where Joe could have expected refuge from British tyranny was here in the United States of America.

But what happened when Joe arrived in the land of the free and the home of brave? He was arrested by Ronald Reagan and Edwin Meese at the behest of Margaret Thatcher who demanded his extradition to Britain. In return for performing this favor, Ronald Reagan just received a knighthood from the Queen of England upon the recommendation of Margaret Thatcher despite the fact that article 1, section 9, clause 8 of the United States Constitution specifically states that no person holding any office of profit or trust under the United States shall, without the consent of the Congress, accept "any present, emolument, office, or title, *of any kind whatever* from any king, prince, or foreign state." [Emphasis added.] I am sure that George Washington turned over in his grave in absolute disgust on the day he saw one of his successors accept a knighthood from a successor to George III.

Eventually, a courageous federal district judge in New York City by the name of John Sprizzo ruled that the British were not entitled to the extradition of Joe Doherty because his act was a non-extraditable "political offense" within the meaning of the outstanding U.S.-U.K. extradition treaty. The reason why that exception can be found or has been implied in all of our extradition treaties is that historically the United States of America has never wanted to extradite the foreign equivalents of Washington, Jefferson, and Hamilton back to their oppressors for imprisonment, torture, and murder. Up until the case of Joe Doherty, the United States of America had always been a safe haven for those who sought to make revolution against an unjust and tyrannical sovereign— just like our Founding Fathers, and especially against Britain.

Needless to say, Margaret Thatcher was so enraged by Judge Sprizzo's undoubtedly correct decision that in absolute secrecy she negotiated a special treaty with the Reagan administration expressly for the purpose of returning Joe Doherty to Britain by abolishing America's hallowed "political offense exception" and applying this retroactively to Joe's case. In other words, according to Thatcher, the liberty and freedom of Joe Doherty was such a threat to British colonial occupation of northern Ireland that it demanded a special international agreement with the United States of America to destroy. And Reagan and Meese willingly went along to accommodate Thatcher instead of obeying Judge Sprizzo's order. Who runs this country— Thatcher, or a federal district judge? Joe guessed wrongly.

The Reagan administration then tried to ram this odious treaty through the United States Senate in the dead of night and with a minimum of hearings. Many of you in this audience were involved in the fight against the ratification of the U.S.-U.K. Supplementary Extradition Treaty. All of us involved in this struggle realized full well what was at stake: the freedom of Joe Doherty and the liberation of northern Ireland. In a *Memorandum*[4] I submitted to the Senate Foreign Relations Committee on this subject, I pointed out that this treaty was tantamount to an unconstitutional Bill of Attainder against Joe Doherty under article 1, section 9, clause 3 of the Constitution. Somewhat ironically, that was the same article and section of the U.S. Constitution that Ronald Reagan later violated when he accepted his knighthood from Queen Elizabeth on Thatcher's recommendation.

We all waged a vigorous battle against the ratification of that terrible treaty, and we almost won. But at the last moment, we were betrayed and abandoned by the powerful Irish American Senators who ultimately capitulated to Reagan and Thatcher. And Joe Doherty has been rotting in prison ever since. It is true that Joe's imprisonment is primarily attributable to the base motivations of Thatcher, Reagan and Meese. But we Irish Americans must share some of the blame for his incarceration during the past three years since we lost the extradition treaty battle. We have fought amongst ourselves; we have been divided; we have not united and fought the British together. That has been our problem all along.

Right now, Attorney General Richard Thornburgh has all the power he needs to set Joe free at the stroke of a pen. We must not let Joe down again. We must use the awesome political and economic power of the Irish American community in the United States to obtain the liberty and freedom of Joe Doherty, and ultimately of northern Ireland.

In the event that Thornburgh will not assist us to free Joe, then we must turn to the Congress where large numbers of men and women of Irish descent currently serve in both the House and the Senate. There we can pass a private Bill for the Relief of Joe Doherty provided we have a simple majority in both Houses of Congress.[5] This is because article 1, section 8, clause 4 of the United States Constitution grants Congress the power to "establish a uniform rule of naturalization." The United States Supreme Court has historically interpreted this provision of the Constitution to mean that Congress has the exclusive and plenary power to determine all rules and regulations that are to be applied to aliens in the United States, whether they are here legally or illegally. If the Bush administration will not set Joe free, then the United States Congress has both the right and the duty to do so under the terms of our Constitution.

As long as the British continue to make martyrs of Irish men and women such as Joe Doherty and Mairead Farrell, there will be thousands more rising up on both sides of the Atlantic to free our ancestral homeland from British colonial occupation—just like Washington, Jefferson, and Hamilton. For over 800 years the British have tried everything they could to exterminate the Irish people, to steal Irish land, to destroy our beautiful language, to pervert our great culture, and to abolish our holy religion. For over 800 years, we have passionately fought them at tremendous cost in Irish blood and freedom. We must not abandon our sacred struggle to liberate our nation now. Thanks to courageous men and women like Joe Doherty and Mairead Farrell, Ireland's moment of deliverance is close at hand.

. . . .

I am convinced that I will live to see a free and united Ireland where Protestants and Catholics can live and work together in peace and harmony. But this will only happen when the British leave Ireland and go back to Britain. And that will only happen when the Irish American community in this country unite together and use our awesome political and economic power to force the British out of our ancestral homeland. After over 800 years of the most cruel, brutal, and inhumane form of continued colonial occupation currently known to humankind, it is time for the British to leave Ireland. And it is also time for we Irish Americans to free America's foremost political prisoner: Joe Doherty. Free Joe!

***

Memorandum in Opposition to the Ratification of the Proposed U.S.-U.K. Supplementary Extradition Treaty[6]
August 30, 1985

I.   Introduction

My name is Francis A. Boyle, Professor of Law at the University of Illinois College of Law in Champaign. I am writing to you today in opposition to the Senate giving its advice and consent to the ratification of the proposed U.S.-U.K. Supplementary Extradition Treaty. In my professional judgment, the ratification of this Treaty by the United States government would be inconsistent with its obligations under basic principles of international and domestic law, would illegally involve the United States in the conflict over the current status of Northern Ireland by choosing sides in favor of the position of the Thatcher government, and would ultimately prove to be counterproductive in terms of decreasing the amount of transnational violence committed by members of so-called national liberation movements against the innocent civilian population in Northern Ireland and other troubled areas of the world.

At the outset, I believe it would be advisable for me to say a few words about my academic and professional qualifications that underlie the opinion of law that will be set forth in this Memorandum. . . .

II.   There Is No Generally Accepted Definition for the Word "Terrorism." [Omitted][7]

III.   The Reagan Administration's "War Against International Terrorism" Subverts Due Process of Law. [Omitted]

IV.   The Laws of War Should be Applied to International Terrorists.
[Omitted]

V.   Additional Protocol One (1977) to the Four Geneva Conventions
         of 1949 Solves the Problem. [Omitted]

VI.   IRA Members Who Have Not Violated the Laws of War Are
         Entitled to Political Asylum in the United States.

     Those IRA members seeking refuge in the United States who had conducted military operations against soldiers, convoys, barracks, policemen, or other legitimate military targets have committed no violations of the laws and customs of warfare. Thus, such non-offending IRA members could neither be tried by the United States government nor extradited to Great Britain without violating U.S. obligations under the Third Geneva Convention and Additional Protocol I. Furthermore, under the 1967 Protocol to the U.N. Convention Relating to the Status of Refugees and the U.S. Refugee Act of 1980, such non-offending individuals would be entitled to apply for political asylum here in the United States.
. . .

     For the United States government to ratify the proposed U.S.-U.K. Supplementary Extradition Treaty would clearly be inconsistent with outstanding U.S. obligations under the 1967 U.N. Refugees Protocol and Congress's own 1980 Refugee Act. This is because the Treaty's denial of the traditional "political offense" exception to IRA members who have not committed a violation of the laws and customs of war would result in their extradition to the United Kingdom despite the fact that such non-offending individuals are clearly entitled to political asylum in the United States. Furthermore, even if political asylum is either properly or improperly denied by the Attorney General, at an absolute minimum, pursuant to the separate and independent international legal right of non-refoulement, these non-offending IRA members must not be returned to a country such as the United Kingdom where both their lives and freedoms would clearly be threatened on account of their race, religion, nationality, membership of a particular social group, and political opinion. Moreover, there is absolutely no way the proposed U.S.-U.K. Supplementary Extradition Treaty can be reconciled with these current requirements of both international and U.S. domestic law by means of the Senate attaching reservations, amendments, or understandings to its advice and consent. Therefore, it is respectfully submitted that this Committee should recommend against the ratification of the proposed Treaty *in toto*.

VII.   IRA Members Who Have Violated the Laws of War Should be Prosecuted for War Crimes by Congress Enacting the Required Implementing Legislation under the Geneva Conventions and Protocol. [Omitted]

VIII.   The So-Called IRA Extradition Cases Were Correctly Decided.

In light of the above discussion, the Reagan administration's claim that there is something wrong with the way the political offense exception to the current U.S.-U.K. Extradition Treaty has been applied by U.S. courts is simply not true. For the most part, the federal magistrates or judges hearing requests by the United Kingdom for the extradition of IRA members have generally applied the framework of analysis developed above for distinguishing the legal consequences of attacks upon legitimate military targets from those of attacks upon innocent civilians by members of so-called national liberation movements. When the requested fugitive has been alleged to have committed an offense that is not a violation of the laws and customs of war, the political offense exception has been quite appropriately applied and extradition has been denied. See, for example, the *McMullen, Mackin,* and *Doherty* cases. The fact that an innocent civilian might have been killed or injured incident to such an attack upon a legitimate military target is tragic and regrettable, but it does not constitute a violation of the laws and customs of warfare. On the other hand, when the requested fugitive is alleged to have committed a serious violation of the laws and customs of warfare by perpetrating an indiscriminate attack upon the innocent civilian population, the political offense exception has been denied and extradition has been granted. See, for example, the *Quinn* case and *Eain v. Wilkes,* 641 F. 2d 504 (7th Cir. 1981).

From this perspective it is clear that the political offense exception to the current U.S.-U.K. Extradition Treaty is working precisely in the way that it should work, and therefore that there is no need to amend the current Treaty in light of the non-existence of any problem under its operation. Apparently the Thatcher government does not agree with the good faith interpretations of international and domestic law applied by U.S. courts to the current Extradition Treaty. Once again, however, the correct solution to this problem is not to require our courts to ignore the requirements of both international and domestic law by ratifying this Supplementary Extradition Treaty, but rather for the Thatcher government to bring its policy in Northern Ireland into concordance with the rules of international law.

Until that time, the situation in Northern Ireland will remain an ongoing transnational conflict, and the basic rule of relevant international law is that of non-intervention for third parties. The United States government is obligated to refrain from choosing sides in this conflict in favor of the position of the Thatcher government. Yet by ratifying this Supplementary Extradition Treaty, we will have abandoned all pretense of neutrality and in essence have ratified the questionable Thatcher premise that the IRA is nothing but a gang of common criminals and that the conflict in Northern Ireland is purely a matter of domestic concern for law enforcement authorities alone. In my opinion, and that of most informed observers, nothing could be further from the truth.

IX.   This Treaty Will Operate Like an Unconstitutional Bill of Attainder.

Let me conclude with the following observation in regard to the proposed retroactive effect of this Supplementary Extradition Treaty as found in article 4. In light of Judge Sofaer's[8] testimony and of numerous public statements made by responsible members of the Reagan administration, it is difficult not to conclude that the ratification of this Treaty is specifically intended by the United States government to lead toward the extradition and eventual prosecution and punishment of Mr. Doherty despite the correct decision by Judge Sprizzo that he is entitled to the political offense exception found in the current U.S.-U.K. Extradition Treaty. In my opinion, therefore, the ratification of this Supplementary Extradition Treaty would constitute the functional equivalent of a Bill of Attainder that is specifically prohibited to Congress by Article 9, Section 9, Clause 3 of the Federal Constitution. Indeed, if this proposed Treaty were to be ratified and the United Kingdom were to seek Doherty's extradition thereunder, I would envision a very serious attack upon its constitutionality as applied to Doherty along these lines. It is another black-letter rule of United States law that all United States treaties must be consistent with the terms of the United States Constitution. I would not hazard a guess whether a federal court would hold that this Treaty has operated in a manner analogous to a prohibited Bill of Attainder and therefore is unconstitutional with respect to Mr. Doherty. But I do ask the question, in light of the testimony given by Judge Sofaer before this Committee on August 1, why would the Senate even want to give its advice and consent to a Treaty which the executive branch of government clearly intends to operate as if it were an unconstitutional Bill of Attainder with respect to Mr. Doherty?

In the most unfortunate event that this Committee should recommend that the full Senate give its advice and consent to the proposed U.S.-U.K. Supplementary Extradition Treaty, I would respectfully submit that you recommend the full Senate to amend article 4 along the lines of the note of 8 June 1972 transmitted by the Honorable R. V. Richardson on behalf of the Secretary of State of the United Kingdom, in conjunction with the signing of the current U.S.-U.K. Extradition Treaty of that date:

> It is the understanding of the Government of the United Kingdom that, without prior concurrence by both Governments, no application will be made for the extradition of a person for an offence committed before the Treaty signed today enters into force if extradition of such person for that offence, or any other offence, has previously been denied because the offence was not included in the Extradition Treaty between the United Kingdom and the United States, signed at London on 22 December, 1931.

If such a restriction was thought both necessary by the United States government and acceptable to the government of the United Kingdom in 1972, I cannot understand any good reason that should be responsible for the dramatic change in that policy as found in the 1985 Treaty.

Therefore, article 4 of this Supplementary Extradition Treaty should be amended to the effect that it would not apply to an application for the extradition of a person for an offense committed before the Supplementary Treaty enters into force if extradition of such person for that offense, or any other offense, has previously been denied because the offense was not included in the 8 June 1972 Extradition Treaty between the United Kingdom and the United States. At the very least, such an amendment would eliminate the unconstitutional Bill of Attainder effect the ratification of this proposed Supplementary Extradition Treaty would unquestionably have upon Mr. Doherty. As mentioned above, however, in my professional opinion there is no way the Senate could adequately amend this proposed Treaty in order to remove its most objectionable features under both international and domestic law.

X.   Conclusion

In summation, then, my conclusions are threefold:

First, the Senate Committee on Foreign Relations should recommend against the full Senate giving its advice and consent to the ratification of the proposed U.S.-U.K. Supplementary Extradition Treaty.

Second, the President should recommend that the Senate give its advice and consent to the ratification of Additional Protocol One to the Four Geneva Conventions of 1949.

Third, both Houses of Congress should pass the required implementing legislation necessary to bring the Four Geneva Conventions of 1949 and Additional Protocol One into effect as domestic law.

The ratification of Additional Protocol One and the passage of the required implementing legislation under the Geneva Conventions and Protocol would provide the necessary legal framework for the United States government to deal with the problem of transnational violence committed by members of so-called national liberation organizations against the innocent civilian population in Northern Ireland and elsewhere in the world. By contrast, the ratification of the proposed U.S.-U.K. Supplementary Extradition Treaty would simply constitute a retrograde step that would impede the development of an international consensus along these lines, and, even worse, that would illegally intervene into the conflict over Northern Ireland on the side of the Thatcher government.

. . .

*   *   *   *

A Bill for the relief of JOSEPH PATRICK THOMAS DOHERTY.[9]

Be it enacted by the Senate and House of Representatives of the United States of America in Congress assembled,

SECTION 1. PERMANENT RESIDENCE STATUS FOR **JOSEPH PATRICK THOMAS DOHERTY**.

(a) IN GENERAL.--Subject to subsection (b), for the purposes of the Immigration and Nationality Act, **JOSEPH PATRICK THOMAS DOHERTY** shall be considered to have been lawfully admitted to the United States for permanent residence as of the date of the enactment of this Act upon payment of the required visa fee.

(b) DEADLINE FOR APPLICATION.--Subsection (a) shall apply only if the individual applies to the Attorney General for permanent residence status under such subsection within two years after the date of the enactment of this Act.

(c) REDUCTION IN NUMERICAL LIMITATIONS.--Upon the granting of permanent residence to the individual under subsection (a), the Secretary of State shall instruct the proper officer to deduct one number from the total number of immigrant visas that are made available to natives of the country of the individual's birth under section 203(a) of the Immigration and Nationality Act and, if section 202(e) of such Act is applicable to the country, from the total number of immigrant visas that are made available to natives of the country under such section.

Prepared by
Francis A. Boyle
Professor of International Law
February 5, 1992

*   *   *   *

MEMORANDUM

December 3, 1990

From: Professor Francis A. Boyle

To: Winston Nagan and Paul Hoffman
Board of Directors, AIUSA

Re: Mr. Joseph Patrick Doherty

Dear Winston and Paul:

I am writing to you in your capacity as Members of the Board of Directors of Amnesty International/USA to request assistance by AI and AI/USA on investigating, reporting upon, and somehow rectifying the treatment given to Mr. Joseph Patrick Doherty by the United States Department of Justice during the past seven years. Based upon my extensive familiarity with this case, I have reached the conclusion that the Department of Justice has deprived Mr. Doherty of his right to liberty without due process of law in violation of the Fifth Amendment to the United States Constitution. In addition, the Department of Justice has also deprived Mr. Doherty of rights that have been granted to him by the 1967 Protocol to the United Nations Convention Relating to the Status of Refugees (1951), to which the United States is a party, as well as by the U.S. Refugee Act of 1980, both of which are the "supreme law of the land" according to Article VI of the United States Constitution. Despite the fact that Mr. Doherty's lawyers have won eight separate decisions on his behalf, Mr. Doherty is still being detained without bail in the Metropolitan Correctional Center in New York City for over seven years now.

Indeed, as recently as June 29, 1990, the United States Court of Appeals for the Second Circuit ruled that Mr. Doherty is entitled to apply for political asylum and withholding of deportation under the U.N. Refugees Protocol and the U.S. Refugee Act. Despite this clearcut ruling—which the government refuses to adhere to—on September 4, 1990, the Assistant United States Attorney in charge of handling the case appeared before Federal District Judge Miriam Cedarbaum to oppose Mr. Doherty's request for bail while his political asylum claim is being processed. According to the account of the hearing found in the *New York Times* of September 5, 1990, this Assistant United States Attorney "told Judge Cedarbaum that Mr. Doherty had no constitutional right to due process because he had entered the country illegally as a fugitive from justice in Britain." I find that argument to be astounding, outrageous, and just plain wrong as a matter of both constitutional law

113

and international law. It proves to me that throughout its handling of Mr. Doherty's case, the Department of Justice has been operating upon the erroneous and unacceptable assumption that Mr. Doherty is not in fact and in law entitled to "due process of law" as required by the Fifth Amendment to the United States Constitution.

A long line of case law too numerous to repeat here supports the basic proposition that even aliens who are illegally present in this country are nevertheless entitled to all the protections of due process of law as required by the Fifth Amendment. Likewise, illegal aliens such as Mr. Doherty are also entitled to all the rights granted to them by the U.N. Refugees Protocol and the U.S. Refugee Act. Apparently, the Department of Justice has never cared one whit about the Fifth Amendment, the U.N. Refugees Protocol, and the U.S. Refugee Act when it came to its illegal and abusive treatment of Mr. Doherty. The Department of Justice has now publicly admitted this in a Federal District Court in New York City. **Enough is enough!**

As you probably know from the numerous news media accounts of Mr. Doherty's plight, on May 2, 1980 he and three other members of the Provisional Irish Republican Army were involved in a gun battle with British soldiers in Belfast, Northern Ireland, in which a British soldier was killed. Mr. Doherty was captured, charged with murder, and put on trial before a so-called Diplock Court (i.e., no jury), whose numerous violations of fundamental principles of due process of law have already been established to the satisfaction of the entire international community. During the course of these "proceedings," Mr. Doherty escaped. Nevertheless, the judge convicted him of murder *in absentia* and sentenced him to life imprisonment. Mr. Doherty fled to the United States of America, where he lived and worked peacefully in New York City until June 18, 1983, when he was seized by agents of the Immigration and Naturalization Service and the F.B.I.

Immediately thereafter, the United Kingdom requested Mr. Doherty's extradition. On December 12, 1984, Federal District Judge John Sprizzo ruled that Mr. Doherty's acts in Northern Ireland were "political offenses" within the meaning of the Extradition Treaty between the United States and the United Kingdom, and therefore that Mr. Doherty's extradition was barred. As Judge Sprizzo said: "the facts of this case present the assertion of the political offense exception in its most classic form." *See* 599 F. Supp. at 275-276. Judge Sprizzo's learned decision should have been the end of this matter. Mr. Doherty should have then been set free on bail pending a definitive adjudication of his status in this country.

I will not attempt in this letter to review the tortuous history of litigation that the Department of Justice thereafter inflicted upon Mr. Doherty. But a detailed account can be found in the recent decision by the United States Court of Appeals for the Second Circuit at 908 F.2d 1108 (June 29, 1990). It is important to note, however, that in a November 14, 1988 decision, the Board of Immigration Appeals ruled that Mr. Doherty should be given the opportunity to apply for political asylum and withholding of deportation under the terms of the U.N. Refugees Protocol and the U.S. Refugee Act. In addition, the Board determined that Mr. Doherty had established a prima facie case for relief based upon a well-founded fear of persecution in Northern Ireland. And in its recent decision of June 29, 1990, the Second Circuit ruled that Mr. Doherty is entitled to apply for political asylum and for withholding of deportation. Nevertheless, Mr. Doherty is still being detained in jail upon the basis of the Department of Justice's absurd theory that he is not entitled to due process of law.

Since you are both lawyers, I would encourage you to read the entire Opinion by the Second Circuit in Mr. Doherty's case. When you do, you can only reach the conclusion that Mr. Doherty has been deprived of his constitutional right to due process of law, as well as his rights under the U.N. Refugees Protocol and the U.S. Refugee Act, by the Department of Justice abusing its discretion in the administration of these laws. Indeed, that is precisely what the Second Circuit ruled.

It is very rare for any United States Court of Appeals in a written opinion to soundly criticize the handling of a case by the Department of Justice. And yet the Second Circuit's Opinion is replete with stinging criticisms of the Attorney General's abusive exercise of his discretion in the handling of Mr. Doherty's case. I submit that the Second Circuit's express findings that the Attorney General repeatedly abused his discretion in Mr. Doherty's case are grounds enough alone for Amnesty International to get involved in this matter.

Here I will quote just some of the highly critical language directed by the Second Circuit against the Attorney General's handling of Mr. Doherty's case. For example, the Second Circuit concluded that the Attorney General "abused his discretion in denying Doherty's motion to reopen" his case in order to apply for asylum and for withholding of deportation. The Second Circuit also found that "it was improper for the attorney general to prejudge the merits of Doherty's claim for withholding of deportation without the benefit of a record, and that claim must now proceed to a hearing."

With respect to Mr. Doherty's claim for political asylum under the U.N. Refugees Protocol and the U.S. Refugee Act, the Second Circuit found as follows:

> Despite the attorney general's broad discretion to base other types of immigration decisions on factors such as the government's political and foreign policy interests, our examination of the asylum statute convinces us that congress intended to prevent such factors from influencing asylum cases. In exercising his discretion in this case, Attorney General Thornburgh relied on just such improper factors. We therefore must reverse his order as to the asylum claim as well.

Later on in the Opinion, the Second Circuit had the following critical observations to make about the Department of Justice's handling of Mr. Doherty's case:

> Reviewing Attorney General Thornburgh's decision in light of the above, we conclude that he based his decision in large part on the types of geopolitical concerns that congress intended to eliminate from asylum cases. . . .
>
> . . . .
>
> In giving effect to these [geopolitical] considerations, the attorney general seriously exceeded his discretion. . . . In short, Attorney General Thornburgh exercised his discretion in denying Doherty's application [for asylum] for reasons that congress sought to eliminate from asylum cases, and, in doing so, he abused his discretion.

The Second Circuit concluded its Opinion in the following words:

> In short, it would be unfair to deny a motion to reopen for what amounts to a dubious procedural argument where the alien has otherwise satisfied the standards for reopening *and where the government's own conduct in the case has demonstrated less-than-perfect adherence to procedural formalities.* [Emphasis added.]

Once again, I encourage you to read the entire Second Circuit Opinion. I think the only conclusion you can reach is that the Department of Justice has for several years deprived Mr. Doherty of his right to liberty as guaranteed by the Fifth Amendment to the United States Constitution, as well as his rights under the U.N. Refugees Protocol and the U.S. Refugee Act. Because of this, Mr. Doherty has been unable to obtain relief from imprisonment through the normal administrative and judicial processes. Therefore, I strongly believe that Amnesty International must act immediately, publicly, and decisively in the matter of Mr. Doherty's case.

I look forward to hearing from you as soon as possible on this request.

Yours very truly,

Francis A. Boyle
Professor of Law
Board of Directors
Amnesty International, USA

*   *   *   *

AMNESTY INTERNATIONAL
INTERNATIONAL SECRETARIAT,
1 Easton Street, London WC1X 8DJ,
United Kingdom.

Ref.: TG AMR 51/05/91

Richard Thornburgh
Attorney General of the United States
Constitution Av and Tenth St NW
Washington DC 20530
U S A

4 April 1991

Dear Attorney General Thornburgh
I am writing about the case of Joseph Doherty, a citizen of the United
Kingdom seeking asylum in the United States who is currently held at the
Metropolitan Correctional Centre in New York City.

Amnesty International opposes the return of asylum seekers to
countries where they risk being imprisoned as prisoners of conscience
or subjected to torture, "disappearance" or execution. To ensure that
such persons are protected against return, Amnesty International calls
on governments to ensure and demonstrate adequately that asylum-
seekers have effective access to their country's refugee determination
procedures. To allow governments to place restrictions on access to
refugee determination procedures would be to increase the likelihood
that protection would be denied to those at risk. Moreover, the
determination procedures must be fair and adequate, in terms of being
able impartially and effectively to identify those asylum seekers at risk
of serious human rights violations if returned.

Joseph Doherty is a citizen of the United Kingdom who has
claimed asylum in the United States (US). He was a member of the Irish
Republican Army when, in 1981, he was convicted *in absentia* by a court
in Northern Ireland of murdering a British soldier. He originally claimed
asylum in the US in 1983, but withdrew his claim before it was heard
when it appeared that he would be allowed to travel to the Republic
of Ireland. When this proved impossible, Doherty successfully applied
to the established US authority to re-open his asylum claim. However,
the US Attorney General, Mr. Edwin Meese at that time, intervened
and ordered that Doherty be denied the opportunity to have his claim

118

determined by the established authority. The reasons for this decision included the Attorney General's opinion that it was in the foreign policy interests of the US that Doherty be deported to the United Kingdom. The US Court of Appeals (2nd Circuit) ruled in June 1990 that the Attorney General had abused his discretion in denying Doherty a hearing on the merits of his asylum claim and, among other reasons, cited the Attorney General's improper reliance on the foreign policy interests of the US. The Department of Justice has now appealed this decision to the US Supreme Court.

It is Amnesty International's view that a dangerous precedent would be set if the executive branch of government were allowed, on the grounds of foreign policy considerations, to deny asylum-seekers a hearing on the merits of their asylum claim. In the US, as in any other country, international standards require that the decision as to whether or not asylum should be granted can only be made by the established authority through a fair and adequate procedure. To grant an executive veto on access to the procedures, which is exercised with a view to foreign policy interests, would be wholly contrary to the purpose of refugee determination procedures— that is, the protection of those at risk.

Amnesty International's concern in Joseph Doherty's case is unrelated to the factual basis of his application for asylum. It takes no position on the merits of his claim. Amnesty International is concerned to make known to the US Government its belief that asylum-seekers are entitled to a hearing on the merits of their claim and its objections to the US Government's reliance upon foreign policy considerations in denying an asylum hearing. It is our view that to allow for such a practice would be contrary to international standards and would put in danger many asylum-seekers who are at risk of being imprisoned as prisoners of conscience, or subjected to torture, "disappearance" or execution if returned to the country from which they fled.

> Yours sincerely
> Herve Berger
> Deputy Secretary General

*   *   *   *

AMNESTY INTERNATIONAL
322 Eighth Avenue,
New York, New York   10001   (212) 807-8400
USA

Telex: 666628   Fax: (212) 827-1451

January 31, 1992

The Honorable William P. Barr
Attorney General
United States Department of Justice
Constitution Avenue and 10th Street, N.W.
Washington, D.C. 20530

Dear Mr. Attorney General:

We are writing to you in light of the Supreme Court's recent decision in *Immigration and Naturalization Service v. Joseph Patrick Doherty,* upholding the right of the discretion of the Attorney General to grant or deny a reopening for a hearing on claims for asylum and withholding of deportation. As a result of that decision, you still possess the authority to reopen Mr. Doherty's case, thereby permitting him a hearing on his claims for asylum and withholding of deportation. We urge you to grant Mr. Doherty's request.

Amnesty International opposes the return of refugees to countries where they risk being imprisoned as prisoners of conscience or subjected to torture, "disappearance" or execution. To ensure that such persons are protected against return, Amnesty International calls on governments to ensure that refugees have effective access to their country's refugee determination procedures.

It also is Amnesty International's view that a dangerous precedent would be set if foreign policy considerations are used to deny refugees a hearing on the merits of their claims. International standards require such merits be decided by an established authority through fair and adequate procedures.

Thus, any restrictions placed on access to refugee determination procedures—especially for reasons of foreign policy—would be to increase the likelihood that protection would be denied to those at risk. Such a result would be wholly contrary to international refugee law which is designed to protect refugees from return to countries where they are at risk.

In order to ensure that Mr. Doherty is afforded the protections guaranteed to any refugee, the U.S. Government must permit him the opportunity to fully present his case. Accordingly, we urge that you exercise your authority, as recognized by the Supreme Court, to grant Mr. Doherty a hearing on the merits of his claims.

Respectfully yours,

John G. Healey

Amnesty International is an independent worldwide movement working impartially for the release of all prisoners of conscience, fair and prompt trials for political prisoners and an end to torture and executions. It is funded by donations from its members and supporters throughout the world.

CHAIR, BOARD OF DIRECTORS   EXECUTIVE DIRECTOR

Winston Nagan   John G. Healey

Endnotes

1   *See* Chapter 2.

2   *See* Anthony Nelson, *Joe Doherty and Jackie McDonald Now Working Together*, Irish Echo, March 16-22, 2011, at 10.

3   *See* Brief for *Amici Curiae* Amnesty International and Amnesty International -- USA In Support of Respondent, in *U.S. Department of Justice, Immigration and Naturalization Service, Petitioner v. Joseph Patrick Doherty, Respondent,* U.S. Supreme Court No. 90-925 (October Term, 1990).

4   Relevant excerpts from the Memorandum in Opposition to the Ratification of the Proposed U.S.-U.K. Supplementary Extradition Treaty are reprinted immediately below.

5   I prepared a Draft Bill reprinted immediately below.

6   *Reprinted from* United States and United Kingdom Supplementary Extradition Treaty: Hearings on Treaty Doc. 99-8 Before the Senate Committee on Foreign relations, S.HRG. 99-703, 99th Cong., 1st Sess. 511-33 (1985).

7   Omitted sections of this Memorandum basically follow the argument

in my essay *Preserving the Rule of Law in the War Against International Terrorism*, reprinted in my book **Palestine, Palestinians and International Law** 132 (2003), but with sole and exclusive reference to the I.R.A. as the National Liberation Movement of the Irish People.

8   The U.S. State Department's Legal Adviser.

9   The late, great U.S. Senator Paul Simon of Illinois had agreed to introduce this Draft Bill into the U.S. Senate, which would have postponed Joe Doherty's deportation. But Joe decided that it was time to go home.

CHAPTER FIVE

OPPOSING
THE U.S.-U.K.
EXTRADITION TREATY

Irish America eviscerated Margaret Thatcher's anti-Joe-Doherty 1986 Supplementary Extradition Treaty between the United States and the United Kingdom. The story of how we did so will not be told here because it is now of mere historical interest devoid of operative legal significance. Suffice it to say that thereafter Britain concluded that it would be counterproductive to rely upon the Supplementary Extradition Treaty in order to extradite anyone from the United States for alleged offenses related to resisting imperial Britain's colonial war in Northern Ireland. Consequently, henceforth Britain would choose to rely upon U.S. deportation proceedings in order to get a hold of such individuals for persecution and incarceration as it had done with Joe Doherty.

But from the British perspective, there were two serious downsides to the U.S. deportation process: First, Irish American citizens could be subjected to extradition, but not to deportation. Hence we had effectively placed Irish American citizens living in the United States beyond the reach of Britain's longstanding system for the maladministration and perversion of justice against all Irish.

Second, under international law there is no legal obligation for the United States government to deport anyone to Britain. Deportation proceedings are governed exclusively by United States domestic law. Ultimately U.S. deportation proceedings are subject to the control of the Executive Branch of the United States Federal government unless prevented by a United States Federal Judge. Deportation to Britain was purely a matter of discretion, not legal obligation, on the part of the United States. So Irish America proceeded to exercise its political muscle on the

Executive Branch to make sure that there would be no more deportations of Irish to Britain along the lines of Joe Doherty.

Thus, because he persecuted Joe, Irish Americans mobilized to defeat President George Bush Sr. during his re-election campaign of 1992. Irish America massively supported the election of Bill Clinton under the slogan: "No More Joe Dohertys!" Britain was stymied.

So Perfidious Albion licked its wounds and bided its time for more propitious circumstances to emerge in order to resume its legal vendetta against the Irish and Irish American citizens living in the United States. Empires never forget and never forgive. It would be bad for Imperial Business.

This opportunity for revenge presented itself with the conjunction of two momentous and tragic events in the United States: First came the installation of the congenitally Anglophile George Bush Jr. as President by the United States Supreme Court effective as of January 2001. Second came the terrorist attacks upon the United States of September 11, 2001. Britain exploited this terrible national tragedy in order to try to ram through the United States Senate the most totalitarian extradition treaty ever negotiated and signed in the history of the American Republic. The Empire struck back!

Immediately upon hearing of the existence of this new Extradition Treaty in the spring of 2003 my youngest brother Jerome—a trial lawyer in Chicago like our father before him—and I resolved to set up a National Campaign to defeat it. Eventually almost every Irish American organization in the country joined into a coalition seeking to defeat the proposed U.S.-U.K. Extradition Treaty—along with the American Civil Liberties Union, not surprisingly and to its everlasting credit. Once again Irish America mobilized and organized to defeat British policies targeting our people. It was a campaign not just to maintain the United States of America as a safe haven for anyone to resist Britain's illegal, colonial, genocidal, military occupation of Northern Ireland, but also to uphold and protect the constitutional rights, civil rights, civil liberties, and human rights of all American citizens and residents from extraterritorial British tyranny and oppression.

In a nutshell, the overall objective of the new U.S-U.K. Extradition Treaty by Britain was to criminalize retroactively and without time-limitation all forms of dissent and opposition to its continued occupation of Northern Ireland here in the United States of America irrespective of legal protections afforded by the First, Fourth and Fifth Amendments to the United States Constitution, inter alia. Needless to say, we Americans had fought a Revolutionary War for good cause against the British imperial monarchy for reasons so eloquently explained in our Declaration of Independence on July 4, 1776, the harbinger of America's Constitution and Bill of Rights. It was 1776 all over again. And Irish Americans became the modern incarnation of the Minutemen: The Redcoats were coming!

What follows are the legal documents that were used in this campaign to defeat the Extradition Treaty. These documents are part of what lawyers call the "legislative history" for the U.S.-U.K. Extradition Treaty. Hence they have operative legal significance. In other words, the Ratification Package for the Treaty that was approved by the United States Senate, submitted to Britain, and ultimately endorsed by Britain in the exchange of instruments of ratification for the Treaty, must be interpreted in light of these legal documents.

Irish America's campaign to defeat the 2003 U.S.-U.K. Extradition Treaty held up the final ratification of the treaty for almost four years. Despite our best efforts, the Bush Jr. administration was able to batter the new Extradition Treaty through the U.S. Senate Foreign Relations Committee and then the full United States Senate itself on the bogus pretext that it was needed to fight its self-proclaimed "war" against "international terrorism" despite the fact that it was clearly designed by the British government to terrorize, intimidate, and go after Irish and Irish American citizens and residents who opposed the continuation of Britain's illegal, colonial, genocidal, military occupation regime in Northern Ireland. It was Margaret Thatcher's anti-Joe-Doherty Supplementary Extradition Treaty vendetta all over again and in spades! But two decades later, given the hysterical anti-terrorism political climate in the United States after the terrible tragedy of September 11, 2001, it was no surprise that at the end of the day the Senate gave its constitutionally required Advice and Consent to the Treaty in the fall of 2006. Both the Bush Jr. administration and the British government shamelessly manipulated and exploited the terrible tragedy of September 11th in order to procure it for the British imperial monarchy.

Nevertheless, as a result of our efforts, when the Senate gave its Advice and Consent to the Treaty, the Senate mandated that the Treaty would be subject to a Ratification Package consisting of one Understanding, two Declarations, and three Provisos that became integral parts of the Treaty as ultimately accepted by Britain. This Ratification Package is now of operative and binding legal significance. What it meant, in short, is that, contrary to the original Treaty drafted by the Bush Administration, extradition cases will be required to be overseen by US Federal courts rather than being handled by the Executive Branch, and will have to demonstrate Probable Cause (see endnote for the relevant text)[1]. The Senate's Treaty Ratification Package was specifically intended to deal with and accommodate the legal objections raised by Irish America to this Extradition Treaty that are set forth below, and must be interpreted by reference to them.

In addition, and most critically, in its report to the Senate, the Senate Foreign Relations Committee determined that Article 8 of the

Treaty must be interpreted to mean that extradition requests made by Britain to the United States must meet the Probable Cause standard of proof: " For requests made by the United Kingdom to the United States, evidence sufficient to meet the probable cause standard will still be required, as set forth in Article 8(3)(c) of the new Treaty and under applicable U.S. case law."[2] This Probable Cause standard of proof is required by the Fourth Amendment to the United States Constitution: "The right of the people to be secure in their persons, houses, papers, and effects against unreasonable searches and seizures shall not be violated, and no Warrants shall issue but upon probable cause, supported by Oath or affirmation and particularly describing the place to be searched, and the persons or things to be seized."

As originally drafted and signed by the Bush Jr. administration with Britain, Article 8(3)(c) of the Treaty would have only required from Britain: "for requests to the United States, such information as would provide a reasonable basis to believe that the person sought committed the offense for which extradition is requested." This "information as would provide a reasonable basis to believe" standard would have been for far less that the "probable cause" standard mandated by the Fourth Amendment to the U.S. Constitution. Similar to beauty, "information as would provide a reasonable basis to believe" would have been left to the eye of the U.S. governmental beholder: a mere scrap of manufactured evidence, hearsay, hearsay upon hearsay, innuendo, or even an obviously perjured affidavit by a British government official.

Furthermore, according to the Treaty as originally drafted and signed by the Bush Jr. administration with Britain, "information as would provide a reasonable basis to believe" would have been determined by the U.S. executive branch of government and not by a U.S. federal judge sitting in a U.S. Federal Court. This is of particular significance since the U.S. executive branch has been historically, vociferously and irremediably Anglophile and anti-Irish, including and especially the Department of State, the Department of Justice, the F.B.I. the C.I.A, and the White House during Republican administrations. These U.S. executive branch agencies and their respective officials would readily have turned all suspected Irish over sequentially to Britain on the basis of a mere scrap of manufactured evidence, or hearsay, or hearsay upon hearsay, or innuendo, or even an obviously perjured affidavit by a British government official.

The Bush Jr. administration and Britain were attempting to do an end-run around the United States Constitution when it came to persecuting, terrorizing, intimidating and threatening all Irish in the United States, whether U.S. citizens or not. Irish America stopped them dead in their unconstitutional tracks! We preserved the Constitutional requirement of "probable cause" and restored the role of U.S. federal courts and U.S. federal judges to make this determination.

In the process, Irish America upheld the United States Constitution and Bill of Rights as well as the civil rights, civil liberties, and human rights of all people living in America against this totalitarian onslaught launched by the Bush Jr. administration working hand-in-glove with the British imperial monarchy. Furthermore without our efforts, the unvarnished Treaty would have served as a terrible precedent for the Bush Jr. administration and its Executive successors—whether Democrat or Republican—to have concluded similarly totalitarian extradition treaties with other states around the world, whether dictatorships, monarchies, or alleged democracies. Irish America prevented the further consolidation of a police state in the United States by the Bush Jr. administration in the aftermath and under the pretext of 9/11/2001.

On the other side of the Atlantic Ocean, however, Britain's Prime Minister Tony Blair, in the train of Thatcher, reverted to the unrelenting nature of British imperialism by almost immediately enacting the new Extradition Treaty into British domestic law exactly as originally drafted and signed with the Bush Jr. administration, and even before the United States Senate had given its Advice and Consent to the ratification of the Treaty subject to the above-quoted Ratification Package. Prior to this new Extradition Treaty, when seeking to extradite someone from Britain, the United States had to present a "prima facie case" that the individual requested had committed the alleged crime. This Prima Facie Case *standard was more burdensome than the Probable Cause standard for extradition applied by United States Federal Courts in accordance with the Fourth Amendment to the United States Constitution. But under the new Treaty as enacted into British domestic law, that Prima Facie Case standard that the United States government had to meet was lowered to the "information as would provide a reasonable basis to believe" standard that was significantly less than the Probable Cause standard that is Constitutionally required in the United States. Britain has never had a Constitution. All the easier for Britain's imperial monarchy to abuse its "subjects."*

Blair was such a totalitarian at heart that he did not even care one whit about the basic human rights, civil rights, and civil liberties of British citizens and residents being requested for extradition by the United States government on nothing more than "information as would provide a reasonable basis to believe" that a crime had been committed. We Irish Americans successfully protected all Irish and all people living in the United States of America from such massive human rights abuses. But where were the vaunted British NGOs on civil rights, civil liberties, and human rights when needed to protect all people living in Britain from these totalitarian atrocities inflicted upon them by Tony Blair working hand-in-glove with Bush Jr.? Indeed, under the pretext of 9/11/2001, Tony Blair proceeded to set up his own police state in Britain. Of course Britain has always been a police state for Irish.

Pursuant to the terms of the new Extradition Treaty as enacted into British domestic law, the United States government proceeded to request the extradition of British business people whose alleged offenses had nothing at all to do with international terrorism and had everything to do with financial improprieties that should have been prosecuted in Britain. This has now gone on to create an enormous amount of political consternation and human rights concern in Britain— and rightly so. Consequently, the new British Coalition Government consisting of Conservatives and Liberal Democrats that was elected in 2010 has undertaken a formal review of the Treaty with an eye toward its prospective revision.

Under no circumstances will Irish America accept a reduction of the Burden of Proof standard for extradition to Britain to anything less than "Probable Cause." But if at the end of the day the British government wants to reopen the Extradition Treaty in order to guarantee the basic civil rights, civil liberties, and human rights of all people living on both sides of the Atlantic Ocean, we would be happy to sit down with Britain in order to work out a package of amendments to the Treaty that would accomplish this objective. The proverbial ball is now in Britain's court. I will not hold my breath waiting.

In the meantime, Irish America will continue to monitor extradition practices under the Treaty in order to make sure that the British government and the United States government live up to the promises given to us as set forth in the Senate Ratification Package for the Treaty. If there are any extradition abuses inflicted upon any Irish people living in the United States by Britain and/or the United States government, we remain fully prepared to litigate these matters in a United States Federal District Court before a United States Federal Judge—guarantees and protections that Irish America successfully clawed back from Bush Jr. and Tony Blair by means of procuring the Senate Ratification Package to the Treaty.

The documents below attest to the full dimensions of what was at stake.

IRISH AMERICANS AGAINST EXTRADITION

A THREAT TO IRISH-AMERICANS: THE NEW U.S./U.K EXTRADITION TREATY
By Jerome Boyle
The Irish Free Press, July 7, 2003

On March 31, 2003, U.S. Attorney General John Ashcroft and U.K. Home Secretary David Blunkett signed a new treaty providing for extradition between the two countries of persons accused of crimes. The new treaty, which has yet to be ratified by the U.S. Senate, marks an unprecedented departure from two centuries of American extradition practice. America has always been a refuge for those fleeing tyranny overseas, and a "political offense exception" to extradition has been an essential element of every one of our extradition treaties since Thomas Jefferson refused extradition of an opponent of the French Revolution.

Although the new treaty pays lip service to the political offense exception, it removes that essential protection for those seeking refuge on our shores. Worse, it subjects U.S. citizens to extradition based solely on unproven allegations by the British government. Any American active in Irish affairs faces potential detention, and transportation to the United Kingdom, without any proof of guilt, and without judicial review. Never before in its history has the United States government subjected the liberty of its citizens to the whims of a foreign government. In summary, the new treaty:

1. Eliminates the political offense exception for any offense allegedly involving violence or weapons, including any solicitation, conspiracy or attempt to commit such crimes;

2. Transfers responsibility for determining whether the extradition request is politically-motivated from the courts to the executive branch;

3. Allows for extradition even if no U.S. federal law is violated;

4. Eliminates any statute of limitations;

5. Eliminates the need for any showing by the United Kingdom of facts sufficient to show the person requested is guilty of the crime charged—mere unsupported allegations are sufficient;

6. Allows for "provisional arrest" and detention for 60 days upon

request by the United Kingdom;

    7. Allows for seizure of assets by the United Kingdom;

    8. Allows for extradition for one offense, and then subsequent prosecution in the U.K. for an unrelated offense (thus eliminating the time-honored "rule of specialty"); and

    9. Applies retroactively, for offenses allegedly committed even before the ratification of the treaty.

    No Irish American activist is safe if this treaty passes. While the most immediate threat is aimed at those who reject the Good Friday Agreement, this treaty is a threat to political activists across the board. In fact, the treaty appears to be an effort by the U.K. government to set the stage for the breakdown of the G.F.A. , allowing extradition for alleged behavior occurring years ago by activists and organizations.

    Attorney General Ashcroft appears to be trying to slip this treaty through the Senate without fanfare, similar to the strategy used with Joseph Doherty. No more Joe Dohertys! Contact your Senators today and insist that they place a "hold" on this treaty until its full implications can be aired.

        *   *   *   *

ACLU Opposes British-American Extradition Treaty; Says Measure Removes Crucial Due Process Protections

FOR IMMEDIATE RELEASE
Friday, December 19, 2003

WASHINGTON: The American Civil Liberties Union today weighed in against the ratification of a new extradition treaty between the United Kingdom and the United States, saying that the measure contains a number of ill-considered erosions of judicial review and would threaten the due process rights of Americans and others accused of crimes by the British government.

Most troubling, the ACLU said, is the treaty's evisceration of the Judiciary's role in reviewing whether a defendant would receive a fair trial in the U.K. and whether an extradition request was prompted by political, rather than criminal, reasons.

> "As a beacon of freedom in the world, our courts must retain the ability to deny requests for the extradition of political figures targeted because of dissent against their home government," said Timothy Edgar, an ACLU Legislative Counsel. "Unfortunately, this extradition treaty vests that authority in the Justice Department, not an objective judiciary that can ensure the United States renders up terrorists and criminals, not dissidents."

The new treaty was signed by Attorney General John Ashcroft and British Home Secretary David Blunkett on March 31, 2003 and now must be considered by the U.S. Senate before it could take effect. Attorney General Ashcroft announced at the signing ceremony that the new treaty "should serve as a model to the world," and could lead to revising other extradition treaties. The ACLU contends that Senate ratification of this treaty would encourage the administration to pursue extradition treaties with other nations that diminish due process and meaningful judicial review, and urged the Senate to reject ratification.

Specifically, the new treaty eliminates the American judiciary's role in determining whether an extradition request should be denied on the basis of the political offense exception. This centuries-old exception protects Americans and others from political, religious or other impermissible persecution, and prevents the extradition of individuals who would become political prisoners in their home countries. The exception also safeguards American interests by maintaining neutrality in the political affairs of other countries.

The current extradition treaty with the U.K. was adopted in 1972, and was amended in 1986. The new change narrows the political offense exception to exclude serious violent crimes, but ensures that the accused will receive a fair trial in the U.K. Notably, the original version of the 1986 amended treaty contained the same provision as the measure pending in the Senate in 2003, but because of it was unable to initially pass Congressional muster.

If the new treaty were ratified, an American who opposed British policy—for example, an investigative journalist who wrote of police abuses in Northern Ireland for an Irish American newspaper—could face arrest and extradition without having any ability to challenge, in an American court, whether the criminal charges are really a pretext for the punishment on account of race, religion, nationality or political opinion.

The treaty contains other contentious measures. These include provisions that eliminate the statute of limitations as a defense against extradition, allow for "provisional arrests" and detentions, which can last for as long as sixty days with no formal extradition request providing supporting details—and for the treaty to be applied retroactively.

> "America is not a haven for terrorists and those who use violence against innocent civilians," Edgar said. "But the elimination of judicial review for these political offense exceptions is unnecessary to ensure that suspected terrorists face extradition, and would unfairly erode due process protections in America."

*　　　　　　*　　　　　　*　　　　　　*

March 4 , 2004

Honorable Richard G. Lugar, Chairman
Honorable Joseph R. Biden, Ranking Member
Senate Foreign Relations Committee

Re: Proposed United States-United Kingdom Extradition Treaty

Dear Senators Lugar and Biden:

I.

I am in receipt of an undated document entitled "Response by the U.S. Department of State and the U.S. Department of Justice to Points Raised by the *Irish Americans Against Extradition* Petition." I wish to thank you for your kind consideration in obtaining this formal *Response* to some of these concerns about the proposed U.S.-U.K. Extradition Treaty from the Department of State and the Department of Justice. As a preliminary matter, I fully concur with the 18 December 2003 Letter already sent to you by Ms. Laura W. Murphy, Director of the ACLU Washington Legislative Office and Mr. Timothy H. Edgar ACLU Legislative Counsel, which was also sent to all Members of the Senate Foreign Relations Committee on behalf of the American Civil Liberties Union.[3] Articles 2 and 4 of the proposed Treaty will gut, destroy and eliminate the longstanding, time-honored, and well-grounded "political offense" exception to U.S. extradition law and practice in all but the name.

The United States of America was founded by means of a Declaration of Independence and a Revolutionary War fought against the British Crown, with which this proposed Treaty is to be concluded. But under the terms of this proposed Treaty, our Founding Fathers and Mothers such as John Hancock, George Washington, Thomas Jefferson, James Madison, Ben Franklin, John Adams, and Dolly Madison, inter alia, would be extradited to the British Crown for prosecution of their very revolutionary activities that founded the United States of America itself. Because of our Republic's unique historical origins and background, special care, concern, attention, and consideration must be taken with respect to the conclusion of any extradition treaty between the United States of America and the British Crown.

II.

It is obvious from the text of this proposed Treaty that it is directed primarily against Irish American citizens engaged in the lawful exercise of their constitutional rights under the First Amendment to the United States Constitution in order to protest the longstanding military occupation of six counties in Ireland by the British Crown in violation of the international legal right of the Irish People to self-determination as well as of the United Nations Declaration on the Granting of Independence to Colonial Countries and Territories, Resolution 1514(XV) of 14 December 1960, which constitutes customary international law and *jus cogens. See* Francis A. Boyle, *The Decolonization of Northern Ireland*, 4 Asian Yearbook of International Law 25-46 (1995), a copy of which is attached. In particular, the inchoate crimes specified in article 2(2) and article 4(2)(g) of the proposed Treaty would make extraditable to the British Crown Irish American citizens who are exercising their rights under the First Amendment to the United States Constitution to protest the continued British military occupation of these six counties in Ireland as well as the deplorable human rights violations that have historically been inflicted by the British Crown upon Irish Catholics living in the north of Ireland, in the rest of Ireland, as well as within Great Britain itself and elsewhere.

Moreover, because of the court-stripping provisions found in article 2(4), article 2(5), article 4(3), article 4(4), article 5(3), article 7, article 18(1)(c), and article 18(2) of the proposed Treaty, there would be no judicial review by a U.S. Federal Court of the exercise of such First Amendment rights under the U.S. Constitution by Irish American citizens, and thus this proposed Treaty would be unconstitutional for that reason as well. Under the terms of this proposed Treaty, the First Amendment rights of Irish American citizens would be subjected to the unfettered discretion and political biases of Executive Branch officials who in the past have shown no respect for the First Amendment rights of Irish American citizens when it came to the former's infiltration, investigation, prosecution, and persecution of perfectly lawful Irish American citizens as well as Irish American humanitarian organizations and Irish American political groups who were only exercising their First Amendment rights under the U.S. Constitution in order to protest the longstanding military occupation of six counties in Ireland by the British Crown as well as its campaign of human rights atrocities against Irish Catholics.

Moreover, the unconstitutional retroactivity of the proposed Treaty as set forth in article 22 would render Irish American citizens subject to extradition to the British Crown for their perfectly lawful exercise of First Amendment rights under the U.S. Constitution going all the way back into the indefinite past to at least the 1916 Irish Revolution for Independence against the same British Crown with which this proposed Treaty is to be concluded. This conclusion is only further confirmed and strengthened by article 6 of the proposed Treaty that unconstitutionally purports to eliminate any Statute of Limitations requirement for extradition as well.

Furthermore, such Irish American citizens would be subjected to unconstitutional preventative detention under article 12 of the proposed Treaty at the behest of the British Crown in violation of the Fifth Amendment and the Eighth Amendment to the United States Constitution. Furthermore, such Irish American citizens could be unconstitutionally seized and incarcerated pursuant to article 8(3)(c) and article 12 of the proposed Treaty at the behest of the British Crown in violation of the U.S. Constitution's Fourth Amendment prohibition on "unreasonable searches and seizures" as well as the Fourth Amendment requirement of "probable cause" for the issue of any warrants related thereto. Furthermore, such Irish American citizens would have their property unconstitutionally confiscated and transferred to the British Crown pursuant to article 16 of the proposed Treaty at the behest of the British Crown itself in violation of the "due process of law" requirement of the Fifth Amendment to the United States Constitution.

Furthermore, article 18 of the proposed Treaty eliminates in all but name the longstanding, time-honored and well-grounded Rule of Specialty for such Irish American citizens. In addition, article 18(2) of the proposed Treaty would permit Irish American citizens extradited to Britain then to be summarily shipped onward to some undesignated third state at the order of the British Crown and the political whim of the Department of State, where such Irish American citizens could readily be persecuted by that indeterminate third state. It becomes crystal clear that the primary purpose of this proposed Treaty is for the British Crown to target, threaten, intimidate, harass, persecute and terrorize Irish American citizens for exercising their First Amendment rights under the United States Constitution.

III.

Weighing most decisively against approving this proposed Treaty is the fact that since the U.S.-U.K. Supplementary Extradition Treaty came into force in 1986, the United States became a contracting party to the International Covenant on Civil and Political Rights in 1992, to which the United Kingdom is also a contracting party. This proposed U.S.-U.K. Extradition Treaty will violate several fundamental provisions of the Covenant that are expressly designed to protect the basic human rights of Irish American citizens, inter alia. In particular, but not limited to, I respectfully call to your attention the following treaty obligations and human rights protections under the Covenant that will be violated by this proposed Treaty:

> Article 2(1): "Each State Party to the present Covenant undertakes to respect and to ensure to all individuals within its territory and subject to its jurisdiction the rights recognized in the present Covenant, without distinction of any kind, such as race, colour, sex, language, religion, political or other opinion, national or social origin, property, birth or other status."

> Article 2(2): "Each State Party to the present Covenant undertakes: To ensure that any person whose rights or freedoms as herein recognized are violated shall have an effective remedy, notwithstanding that the violation has been committed by persons acting in an official capacity;

> > I. To ensure that any person claiming such a remedy shall have his right thereto determined by competent judicial, administrative or legislative authorities, or by any other competent authority provided for by the legal system of the State, and to develop the possibilities of judicial remedy;
> >
> > II. To ensure that the competent authorities shall enforce such remedies when granted."

> Article 9(1): "Everyone has the right to liberty and security of person."

> Article 9(1): "No one shall be subjected to arbitrary arrest or detention."

> Article 9(3): "Anyone arrested or detained on a criminal charge shall be brought promptly before a judge or other officer authorized by law to exercise judicial power and shall be entitled to trial within a reasonable time or to release."

> Article 9(3): "It shall not be the general rule that persons awaiting trial shall be detained in custody,

but release may be subject to guarantees to appear for trial. . . ."

Article 9(4): "Anyone who is deprived of his liberty by arrest or detention shall be entitled to take proceedings before a court, in order that the court may decide without delay on the lawfulness of his detention and order his release if the detention is not lawful."

Article 9(5): "Anyone who has been the victim of unlawful arrest or detention shall have an enforceable right to compensation."

Article 10(1): "All persons deprived of their liberty shall be treated with humanity and with respect for the inherent dignity of the human person."

Article 14(1): "All persons shall be equal before the courts and tribunals. In the determination of any criminal charge against him, or of his rights and obligations in a suit at law, everyone shall be entitled to a fair and public hearing by a competent, independent and impartial tribunal established by law."

Article 14(2): "Everyone charged with a criminal offence shall have the right to be presumed innocent until proved guilty according to law."

Article 14(7): "No one shall be liable to be tried or punished again for an offence for which he has already been finally convicted or acquitted in accordance with the law and penal procedure of each country."

Article 15(1): "No one shall be held guilty of any criminal offence on account of any act or omission which did not constitute a criminal offence, under national or international law, at the time when it was committed."

Article 17(1): "No one shall be subjected to arbitrary or unlawful interference with his privacy, family, home, or correspondence, nor to unlawful attacks on his honour and reputation."

Article 18(1): "Everyone shall have the right to freedom of thought, conscience and religion. This right shall include freedom to have or to adopt a religion or belief of his choice, and freedom, either individually or in community with others and in public or private, to manifest his religion or belief in worship, observance, practice and teaching."

Article 19(1): "Everyone shall have the right to hold opinions without interference."

Article 19(2): "Everyone shall have the right to freedom of expression; this right shall include freedom to seek, receive and impart information and ideas of all kinds, regardless of frontiers, either orally, in writing or in print, in the form of art, or through any other media of his choice."

Article 21: "The right of peaceful assembly shall be recognized."

Article 22(1): "Everyone shall have the right to freedom of association with others. . ."

If the Senate were to consent to this proposed Extradition Treaty with the British Crown, that would effectively abrogate, violate, and set at naught these most basic human rights of Irish American citizens under the Covenant, to which the United States is a contracting party. Furthermore, Senate consent would also place the United States of America in breach of its solemn treaty obligations under these provisions of the International Covenant on Civil and Political Rights with respect to all the other contracting states parties as well. Such violations will render the United States subject to the treaty enforcement mechanisms of the Covenant as well as to the other ordinary enforcement mechanisms, remedies, and sanctions for violating a solemnly concluded international human rights treaty as well as the basic principle of customary international law and *jus cogens* that *pacta sunt servanda*.

IV.

Most significantly, on 18 December 2001 the British Crown formally derogated from its obligations under article 9 of the Covenant, whereas the United States of America has not so derogated. So long as that U.K. derogation to article 9 of the Covenant remains in force, there is no way the United States can lawfully extradite any Irish American citizen to the British Crown pursuant to the terms of this proposed Treaty without the United States government violating its own obligations under article 2(1) of the Covenant: "Each State Party to the present Covenant undertakes to respect and to ensure to all individuals within its territory and subject to its jurisdiction the rights recognized in the present Covenant. . . ." The United States cannot lawfully extradite Irish American citizens to the British Crown, which has derogated from its obligations under Covenant article 9, without the United States itself violating Covenant article 2(1) and article 9 with respect to its own Irish American citizens and also with respect to all the other contracting states parties to the Covenant.

Furthermore, as a contacting party to the Covenant, the United States is currently under an obligation not to extradite Irish American citizens to the United Kingdom where they will be subjected to gross and repeated violations of their most basic human rights by the British Crown. These facts have been most recently documented by the Nobel Peace Prize Winning Amnesty International, whose Headquarters and International Secretariat are located in London, the capital of the United Kingdom. Since Amnesty International is right there on the spot, they certainly know of what they speak. *See* International Secretariat of Amnesty International, *United Kingdom: Scrap Internment*, AI Index: EUR 45/008/2004 (23 Feb. 2004); Amnesty International, *United Kingdom: A Shadow Criminal Justice System*, AI Index: EUR 45/030/2003 (Public), News Service No: 278 (11 Dec. 2003); Amnesty International, *United Kingdom: Justice Perverted Under the Anti-Terrorism, Crime and Security Act 2001*, AI Index: EUR 45/ 029/2003 (11 Dec. 2003); Amnesty International Press Release, *UK.: Basic Rights Denied After 11 September*, ENGEUR 45019 2002 (25 Feb. 2004); Amnesty International, *United Kingdom: Rights Denied: The UK's Response to 11 September 2001*, AI Index: EUR 45/016/2002 (5 Sept. 2002); Amnesty International, *United Kingdom: Amnesty International's Memorandum to the UK Government on Part 4 of the Anti-terrorism, Crime and Security Act 2001*, AI Index: EUR 45/017/2002 (5 Sept.2002).

In light of this most extensive documentation by Amnesty International of massive violations of the most basic human rights of foreigners by the British Crown under the International Covenant on Civil and Political Rights, to which the United States is a contracting party, under the European Convention on Human Rights, under the U.N. Convention against Torture and Other Cruel, Inhuman or Degrading Treatment or

Punishment, to which the United States is a contracting party, and under other basic sources of both customary and conventional international human rights law too numerous to list here but identified, analyzed, and condemned authoritatively by the International Secretariat of Amnesty International headquartered in London itself, now is certainly not the time for the United States to conclude this proposed Extradition Treaty with the British Crown. According to Amnesty International, there currently exists a grave human rights emergency for foreigners in the United Kingdom that is quickly degenerating into a human rights catastrophe. Certainly the United States Senate must not subject Irish American citizens to these massive violations of their most fundamental human rights currently being inflicted on a daily basis by the British Crown against foreigners, as authoritatively documented by Amnesty International itself. And the human rights emergency/catastrophe in the United Kingdom for foreigners is getting worse every day. *See, e.g.*, Alan Cowell, *Britain, Citing Terrorist Threat, Plans to Expand Its Spy Agency*, New York Times, Feb. 26, 2004 (U.K. government proposals for secret trials and reducing the "proof beyond a reasonable doubt" standard for criminal convictions). The United States Senate must not risk subjecting Irish American citizens to secret trials, kangaroo courts, and a less-than-reasonable-doubt standard for criminal convictions by the British Crown. The odious infamy of Britain's Star-Chamber and Diplock Courts shall live forever in the annals of American Jurisprudence.

V.

Finally, even if the U.S. Senate were to amend article 3 of the proposed Treaty so as to prohibit the extradition of U.S. nationals thereunder to the British Crown, the above objections to the proposed Treaty would apply *pari passu* with respect to foreigners present in the United States whose extradition might be sought under the terms of the new Treaty by the British Crown, and especially for those foreigners of Irish Descent. The proposed Treaty would violate the most basic human rights of foreigners present in the United States, and especially those of Irish Descent, under the International Covenant on Civil and Political Rights. Covenant article 2(1) provides that the Covenant protects the basic human rights of everyone living in the United States, both citizens and foreigners alike: "Each State Party to the present Covenant undertakes to respect and to ensure to all individuals within its territory and subject to its jurisdiction the rights recognized in the present Covenant, without distinction of any kind, such as race, colour, sex, language, religion, political or other opinion, national or social origin, property, birth or other status." The same can be said for those basic protections of the

United States Constitution mentioned above, which apply equally to U.S. citizens and foreigners present in the United States.

Furthermore, with respect to those foreigners present in the United States, and especially those of Irish Descent, the proposed Treaty would also violate the solemn U.S. dual obligations of both (1) asylum and (2) non-refoulement as required by the 1967 U.N. Refugees Protocol, to which the United States is a contracting party, as well as under customary international law. We must never forget the grave injustices that the British Crown inflicted upon Joe Doherty with the support of the Department of State and the Department of Justice. *See United States and United Kingdom Supplementary Extradition Treaty: Hearings on Treaty Doc. 99-8 Before the Senate Committee on Foreign Relations*, S.HRG. 99-703, 99th Cong., 1st Sess. 511 (1985). There must be no more Joe Dohertys!

Conclusion

For all of these reasons then, the United States Senate must refuse to give its advice and consent to the proposed U.S.-U.K. Extradition Treaty for any reason. There is no way this proposed Treaty can be salvaged by attaching any package of Amendments, Reservations, Declarations, and Understandings. The Senate Foreign Relations Committee must reject this Treaty outright. The currently existing bilateral and multilateral extradition treaty regime between the United States and the British Crown is more than sufficient to secure the prosecution or extradition of alleged terrorists. This proposed Treaty will only secure and guarantee the persecution of Irish American citizens, voters, and tax-payers by the British Crown. This proposed Treaty will also secure and guarantee the persecution of foreigners of Irish Descent present in the United States by the British Crown. The perfidy of this proposed Treaty cannot be overstated or underestimated. This Treaty is a British dagger pointed at the heart of Irish America.

Yours very truly,

Francis A. Boyle
Professor of Law
Board of Directors, Amnesty International USA (1988-92)
cc: The Honorable Members of the U.S. Senate Foreign Relations Committee

**Joint Letter From Irish American Organizations
Opposing US Senate Extradition Treaty**

The following letter was issued today and will be hand delivered to the Senate by Judge Andrew Somers, National President of the Irish American Unity Conference:

JOINT LETTER FROM IRISH AMERICAN ORGANIZATIONS OPPOSING U.S. SENATE EXTRADITION TREATY WITH GREAT BRITAIN AND NORTHERN IRELAND

May 4, 2004

Honorable Richard G. Lugar, Chairman
U.S. Senate Committee on Foreign Relations
Dirksen Senate Office Building
Washington, DC 20510-6225

Honorable Joseph R. Biden,
Ranking Member U.S. Senate Committee on Foreign
Relations Dirksen Senate Office Building
Washington, DC 20510-6225

Re: Treaty No. 108-23, US-UK Extradition Treaty

Dear Senators Lugar and Biden,

On behalf of the undersigned Irish American organizations constituting tens of thousands of members, we urge you to oppose ratification of the fatally flawed US-UK extradition treaty recently transmitted to the Senate.

This treaty threatens the fundamental due process rights of Americans and endangers the liberty of Irish nationals who reside in our country who will find themselves accused of crimes by the British government that constitute valid political activity.

Under the terms of the existing treaty, our courts have ably and justly evaluated extradition requests for political offenses submitted by the British government, a foreign power that once forcibly ruled our country.

We are particularly concerned about the proposed elimination of the existing role of our American judiciary in evaluating political offense exception claims. This exception has protected Americans and others from the earliest days of our Republic by prohibiting extradition for politically grounded activities. Under the new treaty as drafted, an extradition request from the British government could be received on one day and a target, regardless of citizenship or the merits of the extradition request, could be forcibly placed on a plane and deposited with the British security forces the very next day. These are the same security forces that presently stand accused of orchestrating collusive murders of its citizens in Northern Ireland for many years and who have successfully stonewalled calls for independent investigations of such misdeeds.

Other alarming provisions of this treaty would allow for its retroactive application; would eliminate the statute of limitations as a defense to an extradition request; and would also allow for so-called "provisional arrests" for up to sixty days without even the submission of a properly supported extradition request.

Our Irish American organizations are staunchly united against this treaty and its signing has already generated extensive criticism from us and other concerned groups. Such criticism and the accompanying publicity will only intensify now that the Senate has formally received transmittal of this document for possible ratification.

If the Senate were to ratify this treaty, it is our well-considered belief that the British Government would likely begin the wholesale harassment of Irish American and other critics of its policies in Northern Ireland by abusing the extradition process. As such, we ask that you and the members of your committee thoroughly scrutinize this document and determine, as we have, that it deserves to be rejected in full by the Senate.

For the foregoing reasons, we respectfully request that the Senate stand in favor of the due process and First Amendment rights of Americans and vote to reject this fatally flawed treaty.

Sincerely,

Judge Andrew Somers (ret.),
National President, Irish American Unity Conference
Ned McGinley,
National President, Ancient Order of Hibernians
Deanna Turner,
National Coordinator, Irish Deportees of America Committee
Edmund Lynch, Esquire,
National Coordinator, Lawyers Alliance for Justice in Ireland
Professor Francis A. Boyle,
Board of Directors, Amnesty International USA (1988-92)
Tom Madigan,
Journalist At Large & Associate Editor/Producer Wild Geese Today
Stephen McCabe, Esquire,
President, Brehon Law Society

Irish Parades Emergency Committee
Jerome Edward Boyle, Esq., Attorney at Law
John McInerney,
President, American Committee for Ulster Justice
Frank Durkan, Esquire,
Chairperson, Americans for a New Irish Agenda
Paul Doris,
National Chair, Irish Northern Aid
Cody McCone, Esquire,
Brehon Law Society of New York
Joseph Jamison,
President, Irish American Labor Coalition
Fr. Sean Mc Manus,
President, Irish National Caucus
Thomas H. Smart,
National President, Emerald Society of Federal Law Enforcement Agencies,
Inc.
cc: Members of the Senate Foreign Relations Committee

Responses to this joint letter may be mailed to:
Judge Andrew Somers (ret.)
National President
Irish American Unity Conference

Ireland unfree shall never be at peace

*   *   *   *

Testimony in Opposition to the Ratification of the
Proposed Extradition Treaty Between the United States
and the United Kingdom (31 March 2003)
by
Professor Francis A. Boyle
Before the Committee on Foreign Relations of the
United States Senate
19 July 2006

Good day. My name is Francis A. Boyle, Professor of Law at the University of Illinois College of Law in Champaign. I have already submitted to the Members of this Committee a detailed Memorandum of Law against the ratification of this proposed Extradition Treaty dated 4 March 2004 that I respectfully request be entered into the formal record of these proceedings together with my written comments here today.

The United States of America was founded by means of a Declaration of Independence and a Revolutionary War fought against the British Monarchy. But under the terms of this proposed Extradition Treaty, our Founding Fathers and Mothers such as John Hancock, George Washington, Thomas Jefferson, James and Dolly Madison would be extradited to the British Monarchy for prosecution, persecution, and execution for the very revolutionary activities that founded the United States of America itself.

Because of this American legacy of revolution against British Tyranny, the U.S. has always provided a safe haven for those seeking refuge on our shores. We have always been wary of efforts by foreign powers to transport Americans and foreigners for prosecution abroad on political charges. Indeed, in the Declaration of Independence, one of the specific complaints against British Tyranny made by Thomas Jefferson himself was directed at the British outrage of "transporting us beyond seas to be tried for pretended offences." Such is the case for this Treaty!

For that reason, several episodes in the early history of our Republic, such as that of Citizen Genet under Thomas Jefferson, laid the foundation for the uniquely American notion of the "political offense exception" to extradition. In essence, the political offense exception holds that people in the United States will not be handed over to foreign governments for criminal prosecution when the crime alleged is political in nature.

The political offense exception has since become a standard part of public international law. But the political offense exception is not some abstract notion created by the World Court, or the United Nations, or any other international body. It began right here in the United States of America – ". . . the land of the free, and the home of the brave." And it was created by our Founding Fathers and Mothers who knew, from personal experience, that it was outrageously unfair for a state to hand a person over to another state for political prosecution and persecution. It is a bedrock principle of American Justice.

This basic principle of American Justice is now under assault by means of this Treaty which surely has George Washington, Thomas Jefferson as well as James and Dolly Madison turning over in their graves. This new Treaty marks an unprecedented departure from two centuries of American extradition practice. Although the new Treaty pays lip-service to the political offense exception, it effectively eliminates the political offense exception for all practical purposes.

For example, the political offense exception is eliminated for any offense allegedly involving violence or weapons, including any solicitation, conspiracy, or attempt to commit such crimes. As we have repeatedly seen in Chicago, Florida, and New York, inter alia, undercover government agents infiltrate peaceful Irish American groups, suggest criminal activity to them, and then falsely claim that innocent members of these groups agreed with their suggestions. That is all it takes for a conspiracy to be extraditable under this proposed Treaty.

Even worse yet, all it would take for any of the people in this room to get extradited under this proposed Treaty is a false allegation from the British Monarchy that one of its spies overheard them say something reckless about weapons or the armed struggle in Ireland. This Treaty is unconstitutional under the First Amendment to the United States Constitution, which Britain does not have. Indeed, we Americans fought a bitter Revolutionary War against the British Monarchy in order to establish our own Constitution and Bill of Rights, neither of which Britain has.

Under the terms of this proposed Treaty, it would be the politicians and diplomats at the U.S. Department of State, not a United States Federal Judge, who would be adjudicating the First Amendment Rights of Irish American Citizens, Voters, and Taxpayers. My 4 March 2004 Memorandum to you has already identified several other constitutional protections set forth in our American Bill of Rights that will be violated by this proposed Extradition Treaty with the British Monarchy that I will not review now but respectfully incorporate by reference.

In addition, this proposed Treaty wipes out a number of constitutional and procedural safeguards. It eliminates any statute of limitations, unconstitutionally eliminates the need for any showing of probable cause, permits unconstitutional indefinite preventive detention, applies retroactively to offenses allegedly committed before the Treaty's ratification, eliminates the time-honored Rule of Specialty in all but name, allows for the unconstitutional seizure of assets, and permits extradition under Article 2(4) for conduct that is perfectly lawful in the United States. This Treaty retroactively criminalizes perfectly lawful conduct in violation of the constitutional prohibition on Ex Post Facto laws set forth in Article I, Section 9 of the U.S. Constitution as well as the basic principles of public international law and human rights and jus cogens known as *nullum crimen sine lege, nulla poena sine lege* – no crime without law, no punishment without law. Under this Treaty, the heirs of George Washington could have their assets seized as proceeds of a criminal terrorist conspiracy.

Most outrageously, responsibility for determining whether a prosecution is politically motivated is transferred from the U.S. Federal Courts to the executive branch of government. This means that instead of having your day in court, before a neutral Federal Judge, you will be required to rely on the not-so-tender mercies of the Department of State, which historically has always been soundly Anglophile, pro-British, anti-Irish, and against Irish Americans and Irish America. There are now over twenty million Irish American Citizens, Voters, and Taxpayers, and we all especially like to vote. These and the several other court-stripping provisions of this proposed Treaty are unconstitutional under Article III of the United States Constitution.

As the current U.S. Irish deportation cases show, Britain can easily return Irish and British citizens to Britain. So why is the British Monarchy now trying now to shift the extradition decision from the U.S. Federal Courts to the executive branch? Because you cannot deport a U.S. citizen. A U.S. citizen has to be extradited. Article 3 of the proposed Treaty makes it crystal clear that the British Monarchy wants to target Irish American Citizens for persecution in Crown courts, which have a long history of perpetrating legal atrocities against innocent Irish People. That is precisely why the U.S. Senate deliberately put the so-called Rule of Inquiry by a U.S. Federal Judge into Article 3 of the 1986 Supplementary Extradition Treaty with Britain. This proposed Treaty eliminates the Senate's well-grounded Rule of Inquiry to prevent British Crown courts mistreating Irish People.

Furthermore, unlike Article VIIIbis of the proposed Extradition Protocol with Israel, for some mysterious and unexplained reason Article 6 of the proposed Extradition Treaty with the British Monarchy eliminates any statute of limitations requirements. So citizens of Israel get to benefit from a statute of limitations, but Irish American Citizens of the United States do not. Why this differential treatment on behalf of foreigners and against Irish American Citizens in these two simultaneously proposed

Extradition Treaties?

The answer to this question becomes quite clear in Article 2(2) and Article 4(2)(g) of the proposed Extradition Treaty with the British Monarchy, which renders extraditable an accessory after the fact to an extraditable offense. Since there are no statute of limitations requirements and the proposed Treaty is retroactive, any Irish American Citizen who provided assistance to Joe Doherty would today be extraditable under this proposed Treaty as an accessory after the fact to Mr. Doherty. In addition, such Irish American Doherty supporters would be provisionally arrested and indefinitely detained under Article 12 of the proposed Treaty. Finally, according to Article 16 of the proposed Treaty, such Irish American Doherty supporters would have their homes, businesses, cars, and other property seized, sold and surrendered to the British Monarchy.

That is the real agenda behind this proposed Extradition Treaty with the British Monarchy: British retaliation against Irish American Citizens, Voters and Taxpayers because of our near universal support for Joe Doherty and other I.R.A. soldiers who fled to the United States of America seeking refuge from fighting their own revolution against British Tyranny in Ireland since the Proclamation of the Irish Republic on Easter Sunday 1916. This proposed Treaty has been designed by the British government to eviscerate, overturn, and reverse the delicately crafted human rights compromises that were deliberately built into the 1986 Supplementary Extradition Treaty by the Senate Foreign Relations Committee and other concerned Members of the United States Senate. Will the United States Senate and this Committee permit the British Monarchy to traduce its previous handiwork? I certainly trust not.

Next, for reasons fully explained in my 4 March 2004 Memorandum to you, if the Senate were to consent to this proposed Extradition Treaty, that would effectively abrogate the most basic human rights of Irish American Citizens under the International Covenant on Civil and Political Rights to which the United States is a contracting party. Furthermore, such Senate consent to this proposed Treaty would also place the United States of America in breach of its solemn treaty obligations under numerous provisions of that human rights Covenant with respect to all the other contracting states parties. Such violations will render the United States subject to the treaty enforcement mechanisms of that Covenant as well as to the other ordinary enforcement mechanisms, remedies, and sanctions for violating a solemnly concluded international human rights treaty as well as the basic principle of customary international law and *jus cogens* that *pacta sunt servanda:* i.e., treaties must be obeyed.

My 4 March 2004 Memorandum to you established that the proposed Extradition Treaty will grossly violate this solemn International Human Rights Covenant that has received the advice and consent of 2/3rds of the Members of the United States Senate and is thus "the supreme Law of the Land" under Article VI of the United States Constitution. Nevertheless, the two lawyers from the Departments of State and Justice who appeared before this Committee on 15 November 2005 did not even bother to address these weighty issues of international law, U.S. constitutional law, U.S. treaty law, and basic human rights protections. With all due respect, this Committee must uphold the Senate's constitutional responsibilities and prerogatives under the Treaties Clause in Article II, Section 2 of the U.S. Constitution by demanding that both the Departments of State and Justice formally respond in writing to my 4 March 2004 Memorandum's arguments that this proposed Extradition Treaty will violate the International Covenant on Civil and Political Rights, to which both the United States and the United Kingdom are contracting parties.

Finally, the British Monarchy has continued to maintain a colonial military occupation regime consisting in part of about 15,000 soldiers in the six northeast counties of Ireland in gross violation of the right of the Irish People to self-determination under both customary and conventional international law, including but not limited to Article I(1) of the International Covenant on Civil and Political Rights to which the Republic of Ireland, the United States, and the British Monarchy are all contracting parties. This longstanding instance of British criminality has been analyzed in great detail by my article *The Decolonization of Northern Ireland,* 4 Asian Yearbook of International Law 25-46 (1995), a copy of which is attached. I respectfully request that this article be submitted into the formal record of these proceedings.

All of the above incontestable historical facts provide proof-positive of precisely why this proposed Treaty of Extradition with the British Monarchy must be treated completely differently from any other extradition treaty that the United States of America might have or propose to have with any other country in the world. All of these other so-called modern extradition treaties are historically, politically, and legally inapposite to this proposed Extradition Treaty with the British Monarchy, which obstinately continues illegally to occupy Ireland militarily and to maintain a colony there in blatant violation of the United Nations' seminal Decolonization Resolution of 1960. Furthermore, this Extradition Treaty with the British Monarchy must stand alone and apart from all other modern U.S. extradition treaties precisely because we Americans fought a bitter Revolutionary War against the British Monarchy to found this

Republic. We Americans did not fight a Revolutionary War against any other state in the world. So it is axiomatic that this proposed Treaty with the British Monarchy must be quite carefully distinguished from all of our extradition treaties with every other country in the world -- and rejected!

Conclusion

For all these reasons the Senate Foreign Relations Committee must reject this Treaty outright. There is no way this unconstitutional and illegal treaty can be salvaged by attaching any package of amendments, reservations, declarations, or understandings. The currently existing bilateral and multilateral extradition treaty regime between the United States and the British Monarchy is more than sufficient to secure the extradition of alleged terrorists. This proposed Treaty will only secure and guarantee the persecution of Irish American Citizens, Voters, and Taxpayers by the British Monarchy. Thank you.

Respectfully submitted by,

Francis A. Boyle
Professor of law
Board of Directors,
Amnesty International USA (1988-92)

Attachments:
4 March 2004 Memorandum
4 Asian Y.B. Int'l I. 25-46 (1995)

*   *   *   *

Endnotes

1   VI. Resolution of Advice and Consent to Ratification *Resolved (two-thirds of the Senators present concurring therein),* **SECTION 1. SENATE ADVICE AND CONSENT SUBJECT TO UNDERSTANDING, DECLARATIONS, AND PROVISOS**
The Senate advises and consents to the ratification of the Extradition Treaty between the United States of America and the United Kingdom of Great Britain and Northern Ireland, and related exchanges of letters, signed at Washington on March 31, 2003 (hereinafter in this resolution referred to as the "Treaty") (Treaty Doc. 108-23), subject to the understanding in section 2, the declarations in section 3, and the

provisos in section 4.

SECTION 2. UNDERSTANDING

The advice and consent of the Senate under section 1 is subject to the following understanding:

Under United States law, a United States judge makes a certification of extraditability of a fugitive to the Secretary of State. In the process of making such certification, a United States judge also makes determinations regarding the application of the political offense exception. Accordingly, the United States of America understands that the statement in paragraphs 3 and 4 of Article 4 that "in the United States, the executive branch is the competent authority for the purposes of this Article" applies only to those specific paragraphs of Article 4, and does not alter or affect the role of the United States judiciary in making certifications of extraditability or determinations of the application of the political offense exception.

SECTION 3. DECLARATIONS

The advice and consent of the Senate under section 1 is subject to the following declarations:

Nothing in the Treaty requires or authorizes legislation or other action by the United States of America that is prohibited by the Constitution of the United States.

The Treaty shall be implemented by the United States in accordance with the Constitution of the United States and relevant federal law, including the requirement of a judicial determination of extraditability that is set forth in Title 18 of the United States Code.

SECTION 4. PROVISOS

The advice and consent of the Senate under section 1 is subject to the following provisos:

(1)(A) The Senate is aware that concerns have been expressed that the purpose of the Treaty is to seek the extradition of individuals involved in offenses relating to the conflict in Northern Ireland prior to the Belfast Agreement of April 10, 1998. The Senate understands that the purpose of the Treaty is to strengthen law enforcement cooperation between the United States and the United Kingdom by modernizing the extradition process for all serious offenses and that the Treaty is not intended to reopen issues addressed in the Belfast Agreement, or to impede any further efforts to resolve the conflict in Northern Ireland.

(B) Accordingly, the Senate notes with approval –

(i) the statement of the United Kingdom Secretary

of State for Northern Ireland, made on September 29, 2000, that the United Kingdom does not intend to seek the extradition of individuals who appear to qualify for early release under the Belfast Agreement;

(ii) the letter from the United Kingdom Home Secretary to the United States Attorney General in March 2006, emphasizing that the "new treaty does not change this position in any way," and making clear that the United Kingdom "want[s] to address the anomalous position of those suspected but not yet convicted of terrorism-related offences committed before the Belfast Agreement"; and

(iii) that these policies were reconfirmed in an exchange of letters between the United Kingdom Secretary of State for Northern Ireland and the United States Attorney General in September 2006.

(2)The Senate notes that, as in other recent United States extradition treaties, the Treaty does not address the situation where the fugitive is sought for trial on an offense for which he had previously been acquitted in the Requesting State. The Senate further notes that a United Kingdom domestic law may allow for the retrial in the United Kingdom, in certain limited circumstances, of an individual who has previously been tried and acquitted in that country. In this regard, the Senate understands that under U.S. law and practice a person sought for extradition can present a claim to the Secretary of State that an aspect of foreign law that may permit retrial may result in an unfairness that the Secretary could conclude warrants denial of the extradition request. The Senate urges the Secretary of State to review carefully any such claims made involving a request for extradition that implicates this provision of United Kingdom domestic law.

(3)Not later than one year after entry into force of the Treaty, and annually thereafter for a period of four additional years, the Secretary of State shall submit to the Committee for Foreign Relations of the Senate a report setting forth the following information with respect to the implementation of the Treaty in the previous twelve months:

(A) the number of persons arrested in the United States pursuant to requests from the United Kingdom under the Treaty, including the number of persons subject to provisional arrest; and a summary description of the alleged conduct for which the United Kingdom is seeking extradition;

(B) the number of extradition requests granted; and

the number of extradition requests denied, including
whether the request was denied as a result of a judicial
decision or a decision of the Secretary of State.
(C) the number of instances the person sought for
extradition made a claim to the Secretary of State of
political motivation, unjustifiable delay, or retrial after
acquittal and whether such extradition requests were
denied or granted; and
(D) the number of instances the Secretary granted a
request under Article 18(1)(c).

Extradition Treaty Between the United States of America and the United
Kingdom of Great Britain and Northern Ireland (Treaty Doc. 108-23),
Report from the Senate Committee on Foreign Relations, Exec. Rept.
109-19, 109th Cong., 2d Sess. (Sept. 20, 2006), at 8-14. There is also
official correspondence between the two governments set forth in an
Appendix to the Report by the Senate Committee on Foreign Relations
to the full U.S. Senate that also constitutes an integral part of the Senate
Treaty Ratification Package that must be consulted and considered as
well in the event of any litigation under the Treaty.

2   *Id.* at 3-4.
3   The ACLU's letter on the extradition treaty can be found at: http://www.
       aclu.org/ImmigrantsRights/ImmigrantsRights.cfm?ID=14610&c=22

The MacBride Principles for Northern Ireland

In light of decreasing employment opportunities in Northern Ireland and on a global scale, and in order to guarantee equal access to regional employment the undersigned propose the following equal opportunity/affirmative action principles:

1.   Increasing the representation of individuals from underrepresented religious groups in the workforce including managerial, supervisory, administrative, clerical and technical jobs.
2.   Adequate security for the protection of minority employees both at the workplace and while traveling to and from work.
3.   The banning of provocative religious or political emblems from the workplace.
4.   All job openings should be publicly advertised and special recruitment efforts should be made to attract applicants from underrepresented religious groups.
5.   Layoff, recall, and termination procedures should not, in practice, favor particular religious groups.
6.   The abolition of job reservations, apprenticeship restrictions, and differential employment criteria, which discriminate on the basis of religion or ethnic origin.
7.   The development of training programs that will prepare substantial numbers of current minority employees for skilled jobs, including the expansion of existing programs and the creation of new programs to train, upgrade, and improve the skills of minority employees.
8.   The establishment of procedures to assess, identify, and actively recruit minority employees with potential for further advancement.
9.   The appointment of a senior management staff member to oversee the company's affirmative action efforts and the setting up of timetables to carry out affirmative action principles.

Sean MacBride—Dublin, Ireland
Dr. John Robb—Ballymoney, Northern Ireland
Inez McCormack—Belfast, Northern Ireland
Fr. Brian Brady—Belfast, Northern Ireland

CHAPTER SIX

ADVOCATING THE MACBRIDE PRINCIPLES FOR NORTHERN IRELAND

I wrote the following Tribute to Sean MacBride immediately after and in reaction to his untimely death in 1988 while I was arranging for a meeting of the United Nations Secretary General, Sean, Ramsey Clark, the U.S.S.R. Procurator General Alexander Sukharev and myself in order to further promote Sean's anti-nuclear agenda before the U.N. General Assembly. In 2005 Sean's longtime assistant, Ms. Caitriona Lawlor, published Sean's own memoir covering only about the first half of his extraordinary life under the title That Day's Struggle: A Memoir 1904-1951 (Currach Press, Dublin). Reading through it was like having Sean back with me for only a too few days.

According to the statistics provided to me by my friend Father Sean McManus of the Irish National Caucus in Washington D. C., the MacBride Principles were enacted into law by 18 states of the United States and the District of Columbia, with Virginia adopting a nonbinding resolution in support of the MacBride Principles. Thirty U.S. cities and counties passed MacBride Principles legislation, while 17 U.S. cities and counties passed resolutions endorsing the MacBride Principles. Eighty-eight U.S. companies have agreed in writing to make all lawful efforts to comply with the Fair Employment Practices embodied in the MacBride Principles in their Northern Ireland operations. The MacBride Principles on Northern Ireland became United States Federal Law in 1998.[1] Set forth below is some of the legal work I did to get the MacBride Principles adopted by the State of Illinois.

In addition, I drafted the City of Chicago's MacBride Principles Contract-Compliance Ordinance. I had originally thought it would be a slam-dunk for passage in Irish-friendly Chicago. But Britain intervened with Chicago Mayor Richard M. ("Richie") Daley and Alderman Edward *("Fast Eddie") Burke to derail our Ordinance. Having personally seen him in operation, I doubt very seriously that Richie's father Mayor Dick Daley would have given the British Consul General the time of day on anything related to Ireland. In any event, reprinted below are some of the documents testifying as to how we broke this log-jam by blowing the whistle publicly on their collaboration with Britain. The Chicago City Council then unanimously adopted our MacBride Principles Contract-Compliance Ordinance on February 10, 1993. This all just goes to prove the point that dedicated grassroots activists can indeed beat City Hall.*

Finally, my brother Jerome took the Chicago Ordinance, revised it as an Ordinance for Cook County, Illinois and successfully shepherded it through their Board of Commissioners for final passage on May 16, 1995. Cook County includes Chicago and constitutes the second most populous metropolitan area in the United States after Los Angeles County. I am a lifelong Chicago Blackhawks hockey fan. So this was a "hat-trick" for the MacBride Principles in Illinois: Cook County, Chicago, and the State of Illinois.

The MacBride Principles Campaign was one of the most successful grassroots movements in the modern history of the United States. The British imperial monarchy was systematically and thoroughly defeated, trounced, and humiliated all over the main streets of America. The MacBride Principles Campaign also educated non-Irish Americans about Britain's illegal colonial military occupation regime in Northern Ireland. Today the MacBride Principles Campaign is now serving as a template for the adoption of Resolutions all over the United States by state and local governments calling for the creation of a United Ireland free from Britain's longstanding criminal misrule. Thanks to the MacBride Principles Campaign, "a terrible beauty" has indeed been borne in the United States of America.

Finally, as a direct result of Sean MacBride's herculean anti-nuclear efforts, on December 15, 1994 the United Nations General Assembly adopted Resolution 49/75K, requesting the International Court of Justice "urgently" to render its Advisory Opinion on the following question: "Is the threat or use of nuclear weapons in any circumstances permitted under international law?" In response thereto, on July 8, 1996 the International Court of Justice issued its Advisory Opinion entitled Legality of the Threat or Use Nuclear Weapons. *No point would be served here by providing a detailed, comprehensive analysis of this lengthy World Court Advisory Opinion for I have performed that task in my book* The Criminality of Nuclear Deterrence 162-205 (2002). *But in brief it can truly be said that this anti-nuclear Advisory Opinion by the World Court was Sean MacBride's final and most important gift to all humanity in order to liberate us from the specter of nuclear extinction. R.I.P.*

FRANCIS BOYLE (right) with SEAN MACBRIDE, S.C.
Foreign Minister for the Republic of Ireland,
Nobel Peace Prize Laureate and
Chief of Staff of the Irish Republican Army

In Memory of Sean MacBride (1904-1988)
January 19, 1988

After a brief illness, Sean MacBride died peacefully at his home in Dublin on January 15, 1988, just short of his 84th birthday. Sean had lived a long, full, productive, and illustrious life and in the process became one of the great figures of 20th century history. Yet, as he would be the first to admit, he did not "lick it from a rock," to use an Australian outback expression he favored. His father, Major John MacBride, organized an Irish Brigade that fought against the British in the Boer War. His father later became one of the leaders of the 1916 Easter Rebellion in Ireland and was subsequently executed by the British military. His mother was the famous Maude Gonne, a leading figure for the emancipation of the Irish peasants and in the movement for Irish national independence. Like his parents before him, Sean MacBride became a leader of the Irish revolution for independence against Great Britain.

At the age of twelve, Sean joined the Irish Volunteers, the forerunners of the Irish Republican Army. Sean was first imprisoned at the tender age of 14, to be followed by imprisonments in 1922 and 1930. Sean rose to become Chief of Staff of the Irish Republican Army at the age of 24, and spent nearly twenty years of his life "on the run." He ended his association with the I.R.A. in 1937, and the next year was decorated by the Irish government for his military services in Ireland. Commenting on the current situation in northern Ireland as recently as the International Progress Organization's Geneva Conference on International Terrorism in March of 1987, Sean vigorously declared: "The Irish Republican Army has been the national liberation movement for the Irish people since it was founded in 1916!" Anyone who has spent a significant amount of time in northern Ireland would have a hard time disagreeing with Sean on this point.

In any event, in 1937 Sean put down the rifle and picked up the law. Henceforth, he would continue to fight for freedom, justice, and human rights for all people around the world by exclusively peaceful, nonviolent means. Perhaps it is a general characteristic of the Irish people that after having suffered so much themselves at the hands of the British they can immediately empathize with peoples who are downtrodden and oppressed everywhere: Blacks in southern Africa and the United States, Palestinians in the Middle East, Jews in the Soviet Union, campesinos in Central America, etc. Sean fought for them all. Conversely, the successful struggle for Irish independence provided a stunning example to the 20th century world of an impoverished, oppressed and exploited people throwing off the awesome yoke of British colonial imperialism with their own bare hands. Sean MacBride was one of the great liberators of the Irish people and, as a direct result of that experience, turned his compassion, brilliance, energy, and enthusiasm to the liberation of other peoples around the world and, eventually, of all humanity from the threat of nuclear extinction.

In 1937 Sean took the degree of Barrister at Law. In 1943 he was called to the Inner Bar and became a Senior Counsel, thus holding the record of having become a Senior Counsel in a shorter period of time than any other living member of the Irish Bar. He defended many sensational capital cases and had an extensive practice in the High Court and the Supreme Court of Ireland as well as in Africa and various international courts.

In 1946 Sean founded the Republican Party, and as a result emerged in 1948 as the Minister for External Affairs for Ireland in an interparty government. From the Foreign Affairs Ministry, Sean shifted the primary focus of his attention to the causes of European unity, the promotion of international law, and the protection of human rights. From 1948 to 1951, Sean was Vice President of the Organization for European Economic Cooperation, forerunner to the European Economic Community. In 1950 he served as the President of the Council of Foreign Ministers of the Council of Europe.

From 1963 to 1971, Sean was Secretary-General of the International Commission of Jurists and in 1961 he became one of the co-founders of the Nobel Peace Prize winning Amnesty International, remaining for several years as Chairman of its Executive Committee. From 1968 to 1974, Sean was Chairman of the Executive Committee of the International Peace Bureau in Geneva, and later became its President in 1974. From 1973 to 1976, Sean was elected by the General Assembly of the United Nations to the post of Commissioner for Namibia, the former Southwest Africa, with the rank of Assistant Secretary General of the United Nations.

In 1974 Sean was awarded the Nobel Peace Prize for his work in the field of international human rights. This was followed in 1977 by the Lenin International Peace Prize for his work to end the arms race. In 1978 he received the American Medal of Justice from the United States government; in 1978 the International Institute of Human Rights Medal; in 1980 the UNESCO Medal of Merit; and in 1981 the Dag Hammarskjold Prize. The number of his honorary degrees is too extensive to list here.

Americans owe a special debt of gratitude to Sean for the extensive series of negotiations he held with Iranian government officials over the release of U.S. diplomats held hostage in Teheran starting in 1979. In that year, Sean was appointed President of the International

Commission of Inquiry into the Crimes of the Racist and Apartheid Regime in South Africa. In 1980 Sean became President of the UNESCO International Commission for the Study of Communications Problems and authored the now-famous MacBride Commission Report dealing with the proposed New International Information Order. In 1982 Sean became Chairman of the International Commission to Enquire Into the Reported Violations of International Law by Israel During Its Invasion of the Lebanon. And in 1985 Sean served as Chairman of the London Nuclear Warfare Tribunal.

Despite his declining health and debilitating physical infirmities, Sean continued to work strenuously on these and numerous other projects until the very end of his life. Nevertheless, Sean always remained in full command of his formidable intellectual powers, continuously displaying an almost inhuman willpower to pursue his goals. Yet he never lost that leprechaunish twinkle in his penetrating blue eyes, or his wry sense of personal humor and historical irony. Toward the end of his days, however, the two projects that remained the closest to Sean's heart were the complete abolition of nuclear weapons from the face of the earth and the liberation of northern Ireland from the last vestiges of British colonial occupation.

While in Moscow during the Fall of 1986, Sean authored an *Appeal by Lawyers Against Nuclear War* in conjunction with Alexander Sukharev, Procurator General of the U.S.S.R. and President of the Association of Soviet Lawyers. The operative paragraph of Sean's *Appeal* declared "that the use, for whatever reason, of a nuclear weapon would constitute (a) a violation of international law; (b) a violation of human rights; and (c) a crime against humanity." Sean's *Appeal* concluded with a demand for "the prohibition of nuclear weapons as a first step towards the ultimate goal of general and complete disarmament." Sean's *Appeal* was taken up and sponsored by the International Peace Bureau. Their ultimate objective still remains to obtain the signature of tens of thousands of lawyers around the world upon the *Appeal*; to have the *Appeal* endorsed by the United Nations General Assembly; to have the U.N. General Assembly request an Advisory Opinion from the International Court of Justice as to the complete illegality and criminality of nuclear weapons and nuclear warfare; and finally, to establish an international organization of lawyers to work for the complete abolition of nuclear weapons from the face of the earth. When he died, Sean was preparing for a trip to New York to meet with the Secretary General of the United Nations to arrange for the implementation of his comprehensive anti-nuclear program.

The other project of vital importance to Sean until the end of his life was of course the liberation of northern Ireland from the last vestiges of British colonial imperialism and the reunification of the entire state of Ireland. His concern for the deplorable human rights situation in northern Ireland led Sean to become the chief sponsor of what came to be known as the "MacBride Principles" for northern Ireland in 1984. Modeled along the lines of the Sullivan Principles for South Africa, the MacBride Principles were designed to eliminate the blatant economic discrimination practiced against Irish Catholics in northern Ireland, where over twice as many Catholics as Protestants remain unemployed. When he died, Sean had the pleasure of knowing that five states in the United States of America had endorsed the MacBride Principles by means of legislation requiring, essentially, that they remove their state pension fund investments from U.S. corporations doing business in northern Ireland that do not subscribe to the MacBride Principles. Like the Sullivan Principles before them, the MacBride Principles seem to be gaining general recognition and acceptance by state and local governments all across America. Federal "MacBride legislation" is currently pending before the United States Congress.

Commenting upon the reunification of Ireland, Sean wrote an *Introduction* to Bobby Sands' autobiography, *One Day In My Life* (1983). Robert Sands, M.P., spent the last four and one-half years of his life in the H-Blocks of Long Kesh concentration camp near Belfast. He started a hunger strike on March 8, 1981 in order to protest the Thatcher government's refusal to extend prisoner of war status to captured members of the Irish Republican Army and eventually died on May 5, 1981. At the conclusion of his *Introduction*, Sean wrote approvingly:

> In the early stages of the last decade, Paul Johnson, one of Great Britain's most distinguished journalists, editor of the *Spectator*, and one of Prime Minister Margaret Thatcher's most ardent supporters, wrote in *The New Statesman*:
>
> > *In Ireland over the centuries, we have tried every possible formula: direct rule, indirect rule, genocide, apartheid, puppet parliaments, real parliaments, martial law, civil law, colonisation, land reform, partition. Nothing has worked. The only solution we have not tried is absolute and unconditional withdrawal.*
>
> Why not try it now? It will happen in any event!
>
> With public opinion polls consistently demonstrating that only

25% of the British people want to remain in northern Ireland, this author is fully convinced that he will live to see the termination of British colonial occupation in northern Ireland and the reunification of the Irish state. It is most tragic and unfortunate that Sean cannot live to see that glorious day for whose realization he had worked an entire lifetime to achieve. But he died fully convinced of inevitable victory for the Irish people.

Concerning the threat of nuclear extinction, however, it remains an open question whether any of us will live to see the complete abolition of nuclear weapons from the face of the earth before they exterminate the entire human race. In this regard, Sean established an ambitious anti-nuclear agenda for the next millennium of humankind's parlous existence. It is up to his friends, colleagues, supporters and admirers to carry out Sean's last will and testament for nuclear disarmament.

It was my great pleasure to have first met Sean MacBride in March of 1981, when at my suggestion he gave the 1980-81 David C. Baum Lecture on Civil Rights and Civil Liberties at the University of Illinois College of Law in Champaign. His lecture was entitled *The Enforcement of the International Law of Human Rights*, and was later published in 1981 University of Illinois Law Review 385. For one reason or another, Sean proceeded to request my assistance on several projects over the succeeding years, and I was greatly honored to help him in any way possible. As a short tribute to Sean, and as an indication of the profound influence he exerted upon me both personally and professionally, I thought it would be worthwhile to reprint here documentation related to the last two projects I worked on with him that were mentioned above: The MacBride Principles for Northern Ireland (1984) and Sean MacBride's Appeal by Lawyers Against Nuclear War (1986). Over the years, there were many other projects besides them. But these two were chosen because they concerned the subjects that were the closest to Sean's heart until the moment of his death: the situation in northern Ireland and the abolition of nuclear weapons from the face of the earth.

Quite obviously, it would require a professional biographer to do justice to Sean, and I am sure we can look forward to the production of several formal biographies of him in the not-too-distant future. Unfortunately, however, I will not have the opportunity to undertake that labor of love. Sean made it quite clear that he wanted me to concentrate my time and efforts on resolving the problems of nuclear weapons and northern Ireland (in that order), as well as anything else critical that came up during the interim. To the best of my knowledge, writing an autobiography was never on Sean's extensive list of projects to be completed before he died. Thus, Sean's public record will have to speak for itself.

Memorandum in Support of Illinois House Bill 1374 (1987)
on the MacBride Principles for Northern Ireland

May 8, 1987

I. *Introduction*

My name is Francis A. Boyle, Professor of International Law at the University of Illinois College of Law in Champaign. I am writing today in support of House Bill 1374, 85th General Assembly, State of Illinois (1987) requiring the Comptroller of the State of Illinois to survey United States corporations operating in Northern Ireland in which Illinois pension funds are invested to determine whether such companies adhere to the "MacBride Principles for Northern Ireland," which can be found at the end of this Memorandum. In my professional judgment, the enactment of H.B. 1374 (or its successor) would constitute a positive step toward alleviation of the official and unofficial discrimination that is currently being practiced and tolerated on grounds of religion and political opinion in Northern Ireland against the Catholic population of that province. Furthermore, the enactment of this legislation by the Illinois General Assembly would be fully consistent with international law, United States law, and the laws of the State of Illinois. Finally, the passage of H.B. 1374 would generate some small but very positive momentum toward a peaceful resolution of the fundamental dispute over the ultimate status of Northern Ireland.

For these reasons then, which will be explained in more detail below, I would strongly encourage you to enact H.B. 1374 into law. At the outset of this Memorandum, however, I must point out that I do not write here as a representative of the University of Illinois or of anyone else, but solely in my personal capacity as a recognized expert in the field of international law. Furthermore, I have not been paid, or received, or been promised any form of compensation, remuneration or benefit of any kind by any individual, corporation, group or movement for the composition of this Memorandum.

II. *Employment Discrimination Against Catholics in Northern Ireland*

Before 1976, discrimination by private sector employers in Northern Ireland was not prohibited by either common law or statute. In that year, the British Parliament enacted the Fair Employment (Northern Ireland) Act of 1976 (hereinafter referred to as "FEA") which was supposedly intended to rectify this situation. I do not have the time here to elaborate in detail all the defects of the FEA either as drafted or in practice. Suffice it to say that during the first six years of its existence, the Fair Employment Agency that was established to enforce FEA in

Northern Ireland was somehow able to find only 13 cases of unlawful discrimination. Indeed, the Fair Employment Agency is merely an extension of the Northern Ireland Department of Economic Development and is and has been grievously underfunded, undermanned and under resourced. For example, in the 1986/87 fiscal budget, public funding for the Arts Council in Northern Ireland was 3.3 million British pounds, whereas less than one-tenth of that figure (i.e., 0.3 million British pounds) was allocated for the purpose of eradicating job discrimination.

Therefore, it is not surprising that after ten years of experience under FEA, unemployment for Catholics in Northern Ireland is still twice as high as unemployment for Protestants. Approximately 40% of the Catholic population is unemployed, as compared to 20% of the Protestant population. Catholics also have a greater experience with long-term unemployment. In addition, Catholics tend to be overrepresented in semi-skilled and unskilled occupations as well as in those industries such as construction, which are more susceptible to recession and recurrent high unemployment. Catholics with the same level of academic attainment as Protestants do not secure the same advantages in the job market.

Seventy-one percent of Catholics and only 45% of Protestants live in the less industrialized areas of the province. Catholics account for only 13% of senior civil servants and hold employment in the financial institutions in a ratio of one to five. Catholic male unemployment is two times greater than their Protestant equivalents in almost every district council area of the province. Seventeen of the province's 26 district councils have refused to sign the FEA's innocuous Declaration of Principle and Intent that is supposed to affirm their willingness to practice equality of opportunity with respect to Catholics.

The British government readily admits the above facts, which are taken from official government statistical publications. The British government's bald-faced assertion that discrimination is technically prohibited by the FEA has not been reflected in the past ten years of unemployment statistics for Catholics in Northern Ireland. This deplorable situation makes a mockery of any claim that unilateral steps taken by the British government to eliminate such employment discrimination against Catholics have been effective or will be effective in the immediate future.

For that very reason, the MacBride Principles were formulated to effect a change in those discriminatory employment practices that still substantially disfavor the Catholic population of Northern Ireland. Twenty-four American corporations employing 11% of Ulster's manufacturing work force operate in Northern Ireland. As of 1984, the total value of U.S. investment was approximately $1.2 billion. To the extent that these corporations can be encouraged to implement the MacBride Principles, it would go a long way toward alleviating this substantial degree of economic discrimination practiced against Catholics in Northern Ireland.

Such discrimination on the grounds of religion and political opinion is unacceptable behavior under the most basic norms of international human rights law that have been fully subscribed to by both the United States government and the government of the United Kingdom of Great Britain and Northern Ireland. What follows is a brief review of these relevant standards of international human rights law that indicates the gravity of those British violations as well as the sources of authority for the State of Illinois to act to rectify them with respect to the investment of its own pension funds. Under basic principles of international law and United States constitutional law, the State of Illinois certainly has the right, if not the duty, to make sure that its pension funds are not used to facilitate, or aid and abet, prohibited, illegal and perhaps criminal practices against the Catholic population of Northern Ireland.

III. *The Relevant Standards of International Human Rights Law*
A. The United Nations Charter (1945)

Both the government of the United States of America and the government of the United Kingdom of Great Britain and Northern Ireland are parties to the Charter of the United Nations (1945). For the purposes of United States domestic law, the U.N. Charter is a "treaty" that has received the advice and consent of two-thirds of the United States Senate, and is therefore entitled to the full benefits of the so-called Supremacy Clause found in article 6, clause 2 of the United States Constitution:

> This constitution, and the laws of the United States which
> shall be made in pursuance thereof; and all treaties made,
> or which shall be made, under the authority of the United
> States, shall be *the supreme law of the land*; and the
> judges in every state shall be bound thereby, anything
> in the constitution or laws of any state to the contrary
> notwithstanding.

The MacBride Principles on Northern Ireland are clearly intended to secure compliance by the British government with its obligations under the terms of the United Nations Charter. For that reason, inter alia, the MacBride Principles are fully consistent with America's "supreme law of the land" and therefore with the laws of the State of Illinois.

U.N. Charter article 1(3) provides that the purposes of the United

Nations are: "To achieve international cooperation in . . . promoting and encouraging respect for human rights and for fundamental freedoms for all without distinction as to race, sex, language, or *religion*. . . ." Furthermore, under the terms of U.N. Charter article 56, both the United States government and the British government have pledged themselves to take joint and separate action for the achievement of the purposes set forth in article 55. Article 55(c) includes among these purposes "universal respect for, and observance of, human rights and fundamental freedoms for all without distinction as to race, sex, language, or *religion*." To the extent that the British government has failed to obtain equality and freedom from discrimination for Catholics in Northern Ireland, it has breached its solemn obligations under articles 1, 55, and 56 of the United Nations Charter.

Since the United Nations Charter is a "treaty" within the meaning of the Supremacy Clause of the United States Constitution, the General Assembly of the State of Illinois would certainly be entitled to act in a manner consistent with, and for the express purpose of further advancing, "the supreme law of the land" found in articles 1, 55, and 56 thereof by means of applying the MacBride Principles to its pension fund investments. Indeed, according to the Tenth Amendment of the United States Constitution, the "powers not delegated to the United States by the Constitution nor prohibited by it to the States are reserved to the States respectively or to the people." Unless and until the United States Congress decides affirmatively to enact legislation into law that deals with the situation in Northern Ireland in a manner directly contradictory to the terms of the MacBride Principles, the State of Illinois would remain free to apply the MacBride Principles to determine whether or not to invest its own pension funds in U.S. corporations doing business in Northern Ireland.

B. The Universal Declaration of Human Rights (1948)

The human rights provisions of the United Nations Charter were further elaborated upon and specified by the Universal Declaration of Human Rights, which was adopted by consensus by the United Nations General Assembly in 1948. The Universal Declaration of Human Rights enunciates the basic standards of international human rights law to which all individuals around the world are entitled. Indeed, it is the official position of the United States government that the Universal Declaration of Human Rights is binding upon all states and for the benefit of all people around the world as a matter of customary international law.

With respect to employment discrimination against Catholics in Northern Ireland, the following provisions of the Universal Declaration of Human Rights are directly applicable:

Article 1. All human beings are born free and equal in dignity and rights. They are endowed with reason and conscience and should act towards one another in a spirit of brotherhood.

Article 2. Everyone is entitled to all the rights and freedoms set forth in this Declaration without distinction of any kind, such as race, colour, sex, language, religion, political or other opinion, national or social origin, property, birth or other status.

Article 7. All are equal before the law and are entitled without any discrimination to equal protection of the law. All are entitled to equal protection against any discrimination in violation of this Declaration and against any incitement to such discrimination.

Article 8. Everyone has the right to an effective remedy by the competent national tribunals for acts violating the fundamental rights granted him by the Constitution or by law.

Article 18. Everyone has the right to freedom of thought, conscience and religion; this right includes freedom to change his religion or belief, and freedom, either alone or in community with others and in public or private, to manifest his religion or belief in teaching, practice, worship and observance.

Article 19. Everyone has the right to freedom of opinion and expression; this right includes freedom to hold opinions without interference and to seek, receive and impart information and ideas to any media and regardless of all frontiers.

Article 23.-1. Everyone has the right to work, to free choice of employment, to just and favorable conditions of work and to protection against unemployment.
2. Everyone, without any discrimination, has the right to equal pay for equal work.
3. Everyone who works has the right to just and favorable remuneration ensuring for himself and his family an existence worthy of human dignity, and supplemented, if necessary, by other means of social protection.

Article 25.-1. Everyone has the right to a standard of living adequate for the health and well-being of himself and of his family, including food, clothing, housing and medical care and necessary social services,

Article 26.-1. Everyone has the right to education . . . Technical and professional education shall be made generally available and higher education shall be equally accessible to all on the basis of merit.

Article 29. Everyone is entitled to a social and international order in which the rights and freedoms set forth in this Declaration can be fully realized.

Clearly, the British government's practice and toleration of gross economic discrimination against Catholics in Northern Ireland violates its solemn obligations under these provisions of the Universal Declaration of Human Rights. Consequently, the State of Illinois has a perfect right to apply the MacBride Principles to its own pension fund investments for the express purpose of guaranteeing that Catholics in Northern Ireland are accorded the basic international minimum standard of treatment set forth in the Universal Declaration of Human Rights.

As the United States Supreme Court said in the *Paquete Habana*, 175 U.S. 677 (1900): "International law is part of our law. . . ." In other words, customary international law—including the Universal Declaration of Human Rights—is part of the common law of the United States of America and of the fifty states of the Union, including the State of Illinois. The State of Illinois certainly has the right, if not the duty, to make sure that its own pension funds are used in a manner consistent with the general common law of the United States of America and the State of Illinois. Therefore, the State of Illinois would possess the authority to prevent its pension fund investments from being used for the purpose of furthering the continuation of these discriminatory practices against Northern Ireland Catholics in explicit violation of the Universal Declaration of Human Rights.

C. The Two United Nations Human Rights Covenants (1966)

The treaty obligations of U.N. Charter articles 1, 55 and 56 and the customary international law obligations of the Universal Declaration of Human Rights have been further elaborated upon and specified in the United Nations International Covenant on Economic, Social and Cultural Rights (1966) and the United Nations International Covenant on Civil and Political Rights (1966). The British government is a party to both of these Covenants, and therefore is strictly bound to obey their terms. Furthermore, the United States government has signed both of these

United Nations Human Rights Covenants, and therefore, according to article 18 of the 1969 Vienna Convention on the Law of Treaties, is obliged to refrain from acts that would defeat the object and purpose of these Covenants. A similar obligation would necessarily apply to the States of the Union. Hence, consistent with the terms of the Vienna Convention on the Law of Treaties, the State of Illinois would be under an obligation to make sure that its pension funds are not used for the purpose of facilitating or aiding and abetting violations of these two United Nations Human Rights Covenants against the Catholic population in Northern Ireland.

To begin with, the British government has violated its solemn obligation under article 7 of the International Covenant on Economic, Social and Cultural Rights (1966) with respect to its practice and toleration of economic discrimination against Catholics in Northern Ireland:

Article 7. The States Parties to the present Covenant recognize the right of everyone to the enjoyment of just and favourable conditions of work, which ensure, in particular:
(a) Remuneration which provides all workers as a minimum with:
(i) Fair wages and equal remuneration for work of equal value without distinction of any kind, in particular women being guaranteed conditions of work not inferior to those enjoyed by men, with equal pay for equal work; and
(ii) A decent living for themselves and their families in accordance with the provisions of the present Covenant;
(b) Safe and healthy working conditions;
(c) Equal opportunity for everyone to be promoted in his employment to an appropriate higher level, subject to no considerations other than those of seniority and competence;
(d) Rest, leisure and reasonable limitation of working hours and periodic holidays with pay, as well as remuneration for public holidays.

Also, British practices in Northern Ireland have violated several provisions of the United Nations International Covenant on Civil and Political Rights (1966). According to article 2(1) thereof each party to the Covenant undertakes to respect and to ensure to all individuals within its territory and subject to its jurisdiction the rights recognized in the Covenant "without distinction of any kind such as race, color, sex, language, *religion, political or other opinion,* national or social origin, property, birth or other status." Because of the close connection between politics and religion in Northern Ireland, religious discrimination as a practice is generally acknowledged to be interchangeable with political discrimination.

Furthermore, article 3 requires the British government to ensure the equal right of men and women to the enjoyment of all civil and political rights set forth in this Covenant. According to Covenant article 18(1), everyone in Northern Ireland has the right to freedom of thought, conscience and religion. Clearly, this right would include within itself the right to freedom from discrimination for the practice of the Catholic religion. The same argument would apply to article 19(1) which provides that everyone shall have the right to hold opinions without interference.

Finally, Covenant article 26 provides that all persons are equal before the law and are entitled without any discrimination to equal protection of the law: "In this respect, the law shall prohibit any discrimination and guarantee to all persons equal *and effective protection* against discrimination on any grounds such as race, color, sex, language, *religion, political or other opinion*, national or social origin, property, birth or other status."

The British government has clearly failed to discharge its most elementary obligations under the aforementioned provisions of these two United Nations Human Rights Covenants of 1966 by means of its practicing and tolerating discriminatory treatment against Catholics in Northern Ireland. The MacBride Principles have been designed to induce compliance by the British government with its obligations under these two U.N. Human Rights Covenants. Since the United States government has signed both these Covenants, it would certainly be permissible for the State of Illinois to apply the MacBride Principles to its own pension fund investments in U.S. corporations doing business in Northern Ireland for the express purpose of securing their compliance with the requirements of these Covenants.

C. The European Convention on Human Rights

These solemn treaty and customary international law obligations of the British government have likewise been reiterated in article 14 of the European Convention for the Protection of Human Rights and Fundamental Freedoms (1950), which provides that the enjoyment of the rights and freedoms set forth in this Convention shall be secured "without discrimination on any ground such as sex, race, colour, language, religion, political or other opinion, national or social origin, association with a national minority, property, birth or other status." Article 14 goes beyond the requirements of the aforementioned obligations when it expressly prohibits discrimination on the grounds of "association with a national minority." That is precisely what the British government is permitting to happen to the Catholic population in Northern Ireland today.

D. The Genocide Convention

The final source of international law relevant to the analysis here is the International Convention on the Prevention and Punishment of the Crime of Genocide (1948). The British government is a party to the Genocide Convention; and at the specific request of the Reagan administration, the United States Senate finally gave its advice and consent to this Convention in 1986. Moreover, all reputable professors of international law whom I know of would agree that the Genocide Convention enunciates the basic rules of customary international law binding upon all member states and individuals within the world community, including Representatives and Senators elected to the Illinois General Assembly.

Article 1 of the Genocide Convention provides that genocide, whether committed in time of peace or in time of war, is a crime under international law which the contracting parties *"undertake to prevent and to punish."* The definition of "genocide" can be found in Convention article 2:

> Article II. In the present Convention, genocide means any of the following acts committed with intent to destroy, in whole or in part, a national, ethnical, racial or religious group as such:
> (a) Killing members of the group;
> (b) *Causing serious bodily or mental harm to members of the group;*
> (c) *Deliberately inflicting on the group conditions of life calculated to bring about its physical destruction in whole or in part;*
> (d) Imposing measures intended to prevent births within the group;
> (e) Forcibly transferring children of the group to another group.

In the tragic history of British colonial occupation in Ireland, the British government has committed genocidal practices against the Irish people because of their national, ethnical, racial and religious characteristics as such. The current British policies in Northern Ireland with respect to practicing and condoning such massive economic discrimination against Catholics as such raise serious questions as to governmental responsibility for committing the international crime of genocide as defined by Convention articles 2(b) and 2(c).

Furthermore, Genocide Convention article 3 expressly recognizes the existence of inchoate international crimes with respect to genocide. Hence, conspiracy to commit genocide, direct and public incitement to commit genocide, attempt to commit genocide, and "complicity in genocide" are all international crimes in their own right. Moreover, Genocide Convention article 4 provides that persons committing genocide or any of the inchoate crimes enumerated in article 3 must be punished "whether they are constitutionally responsible rulers, *public officials*, or private individuals." Under the terms of the Genocide Convention, the State of Illinois would have an obligation to investigate and determine whether its pension funds are being used for the purpose of facilitating, or aiding and abetting, genocide against the Catholic population of Northern Ireland as defined by articles 2(b) and 2(c) thereof. In the event that question is answered in the affirmative, the State of Illinois would be obligated to prevent the use of its pension funds for the purpose of facilitating or aiding and abetting genocide against Catholics in Northern Ireland. Otherwise, Illinois public officials could possibly become accomplices to the commission of the international crime of genocide against Catholics in Northern Ireland.

IV. *United States Case Law*

So far, there has been only one United States case dealing with the MacBride Principles, *N.Y. City Employees' Retirement System v. American Brands*, 634 F. Supp. 1382 (S.D.N.Y. 1986) (hereinafter referred to as *NYCER's*). In this case, the plaintiff-shareholder moved for a preliminary injunction requiring the defendant-corporation to include in its management's proxy solicitation materials the plaintiff's proposed implementation of the MacBride Principles. The plaintiff sought to bar the defendant from soliciting proxies at the annual meeting unless it made a supplemental mailing to solicit proxies for the plaintiff's proposal that the MacBride Principles be adopted by defendant's Northern Ireland subsidiary.

Federal District Judge Robert Carter held that the plaintiff-shareholder made a strong showing of likelihood that it could prove that all nine of the MacBride Principles for equal employment practices could be legally implemented by defendant's management in its Northern Ireland factory under British law. In other words, the MacBride Principles did not violate the terms of the aforementioned Fair Employment (Northern Ireland) Act of 1976 (FEA). Judge Carter found that MacBride

Principles 2, 5, and 6 merely restated outstanding requirements under the FEA; that Principles 3 and 9 required action going beyond the requirements of the FEA but did not raise arguable violations of that legislation; and that Principles 1, 4, 7, and 8 may be interpreted as requiring some form of affirmative action programs which generically had already been established or condoned by the Agency in charge of FEA's administration.

The *NYCER's* holding simply confirmed several points that had already been firmly established by the proponents of the MacBride Principles. First, that no American corporation operating in Northern Ireland would ever be expected to violate British law by means of implementing the MacBride Principles. Second, that the MacBride Principles do not require companies to engage in reverse discrimination or to adopt "quotas" for individuals from underrepresented religious groups with respect to hiring. Third, that the MacBride Principles constitute a minimum framework for affirmative action programs and activities that would be fully consistent with the FEA.

I should point out that just recently the United States Supreme Court upheld the validity of an affirmative action program against attack in *Johnson v. Transportation Agency*, 55 U.S.L.W. 4379 (Mar. 25, 1987). On the basis of *NYCER's* and *Johnson*, I would anticipate that the chances of anyone mounting a successful challenge to the constitutionality or legality of H.B. 1374 (or its successor) in a U.S. federal district court or a court of the State of Illinois would be slight and therefore remote. In the unlikely event of such a lawsuit, *NYCER's* upholding of the MacBride Principles would be substantially bolstered by the international law and constitutional law arguments presented in this Memorandum, which were not considered in that case.

V. *Conclusion*

For all of the above reasons, then, I see no problem under international law, United States law, or the laws of the State of Illinois with respect to applying the MacBride Principles to the investment of Illinois pension funds in U.S. corporations doing business in Northern Ireland. In light of the gross and consistent pattern of violations of fundamental human rights law perpetrated by the British government against the Catholic population of Northern Ireland, it is certainly understandable why the advocates of the MacBride Principles would seek to lessen the gravity of these offenses to whatever limited extent possible. In regard to all of the aforementioned treaties (except the European Convention on Human Rights), the United States government is either a party thereto or a signatory thereof. Consequently, under basic principles of international law and United States constitutional law, the State of Illinois would certainly have a right to act in a manner not only consistent with the requirements of these treaties and of customary international law, but also for the express purpose of implementing these international legal obligations to whatever limited extent possible. Unless and until the United States Congress enacts into law legislation that provides expressly to the contrary, the State of Illinois would remain free under the Tenth Amendment of the United States Constitution to apply the MacBride Principles to its own pension fund investments for the express purpose of upholding "the supreme law of the land" as recognized by Article 6 of the United States Constitution and the Supreme Court's *Paquete Habana* decision.

I should point out, however, that H.B. 1374 does not attempt to enact the MacBride Principles into Illinois law at this time. Rather, all this legislation would require is for the Comptroller of the State of Illinois to undertake a survey of United States corporations operating in Northern Ireland in which Illinois pension funds are invested. Clearly, the State of Illinois would have the right, if not the obligation, to investigate and determine whether or not United States corporations operating in Northern Ireland in which Illinois pension funds have been invested are using the capital generated by such investments in a manner consistent with the requirements of international law and treaties as fully subscribed to by the government of the United Kingdom of Great Britain and Northern Ireland and by the government of the United States of America.

In my professional opinion, the State of Illinois must certainly determine whether or not its pension funds are being used for prohibited, illegal, and perhaps criminal purposes in Northern Ireland. As an employee of the State of Illinois, I would definitely not want to see any of my personal pension funds being used for the purpose of facilitating, or aiding and abetting, the commission of international crimes and gross violations of international human rights law against the Catholic population of Northern Ireland. Illinois public officials would obviously not want to become unwitting accomplices to international crimes or other violations of international human rights law committed against Catholics in Northern Ireland.

Indeed, it is a basic principle of Anglo-American criminal law that for the purpose of establishing criminal intent (i.e., *mens rea*), willful ignorance is tantamount to knowledge. Hence, I would respectfully submit that the State of Illinois has an affirmative duty to determine whether or not its pension funds are being used by U.S. corporations in Northern Ireland to facilitate, or aid and abet, prohibited, illegal and perhaps criminal practices against the Catholic population of that province. The enactment of H.B. 1374 into Illinois law would certainly discharge this most rudimentary obligation under the well-recognized principles of international law and U.S. constitutional law discussed above.

Thank you very much for your kind attention to this matter. It has been greatly appreciated. And if you have any further questions, please feel free to get in touch with me directly at 217-333-7954.

Yours very truly,

Francis A. Boyle
Professor of Law

*   *   *   *

June 19, 1987

The Honorable John J. McNamara
Illinois House of Representatives
2040 Stratton Building
Springfield, Illinois 62706

Dear Representative McNamara:

This is to respond to Mr. Roger Carrick's[2] letter to you of June 11, 1987 and his attached critique of my *Memorandum in Support of Illinois House Bill 1374 (1987) on the MacBride Principles for Northern Ireland*, dated May 8, 1987. Unfortunately, Mr. Carrick did not have the courtesy to send me a copy of his letter or the attached critique (hereinafter referred to as the "Carrick Critique"). So I do apologize to you for not having a written response to the Carrick Critique ready on time for the June 16 hearings before the House Committee on State and Government Administration. What follows is a brief summary of and elaboration upon the oral comments on the Carrick Critique that I delivered in my presentation before the Committee that morning:

1. Mr. Carrick began his Critique in paragraph 1 by claiming that my *Memorandum* "is, of course, a political tract with a clear political and religious bias." I have never had the opportunity to meet with or even talk to Mr. Carrick, so I do not believe that he knows anything at all about my political opinions or religious beliefs. I would submit, however, that whatever the latter might be is completely irrelevant to the substance of the legal analysis I presented in my *Memorandum*. Attached you will find a copy of my resumé that details my scholarly credentials and professional activities in the field of international law, which fully support the integrity

of the legal opinion presented in the *Memorandum*. You are certainly free to read the resumé and determine for yourself whether or not I am qualified to give an objective analysis of the principles of international law and international human rights law that pertain to the situation in Northern Ireland. I am the only professor of public international law in the entire University of Illinois system.

2. In light of Mr. Carrick's aspersions on the objectivity of my analysis, however, I should reiterate that I do not represent any government, group, movement, organization, corporation, or individual other than myself in my personal capacity as a recognized expert in the field of international law. By contrast, Mr. Carrick is a paid representative of the Thatcher government, which has publicly taken a strong position against the MacBride Principles for political reasons. The only payroll I am on is that of the University of Illinois College of Law, which is the premier law school in the State of Illinois' educational system. As I had stated at the very outset of my *Memorandum*, I have not been paid one penny by anyone to write the *Memorandum*, or to appear before the House Committee in support of H.B. 1374. Nor have I even received any form of reimbursement for my out-of-pocket expenses incidental to these activities. It is a pity that the same cannot be said for Mr. Carrick or any of his associates who were present at the June 16 hearings. I respectfully suggest that you evaluate his critique of my *Memorandum* in this light.

3. The gist of Mr. Carrick's critique of my *Memorandum* is basically factual in nature. Mr. Carrick and I can quibble about statistics forever. Nevertheless, he readily concedes the one undeniable fact that lies at the very heart of my international law analysis of the human rights situation in Northern Ireland. To quote directly from paragraph 7 of the Carrick Critique: *"The British Government recognizes that Catholic unemployment is still twice as high as that for Protestant: It also recognizes that more needs to be done to accelerate the pace of change."* After eleven years of experience with the toothless Fair Employment Act of 1976, the British Consul General openly and officially admits that there has been no fundamental change in the unemployment ratio between Catholics and Protestants in Northern Ireland. It is my professional opinion that without the impetus provided by the MacBride Principles, the situation will probably be the same eleven years from now as well: Percentagewise, twice as many Catholics will still be unemployed as Protestants. By enacting H.B. 1374 into law, the State of Illinois can significantly "accelerate the pace of change" by encouraging the closure of this enormous, illegal, and unjustifiable gap between Catholic and Protestant unemployment ratios in Northern Ireland.

4. If the Thatcher government genuinely wishes to "accelerate

the pace of change" for Catholic employment in Northern Ireland, then it should vigorously support, not oppose, the MacBride Principles. In this regard it is important to note that the opposition British Labor Party has already taken a strong position in support of the MacBride Principles in a September 1986 *Statement* it submitted to the Northern Ireland Standing Advisory Commission on Human Rights. I ask the following question: Who is playing politics with human rights in Northern Ireland—Thatcher/Carrick or me?

5. Paragraph 17 of the Carrick Critique makes a glancing reference to "*International Human Rights Law.*" You will note that Mr. Carrick made absolutely no attempt whatsoever to refute even one iota of the legal analysis that was provided in my *Memorandum* on the binding nature of the human rights provisions found in the United Nations Charter (1945), the Universal Declaration of Human Rights (1948), the International Covenant on Economic, Social, and Cultural Rights (1966), and the International Covenant on Civil and Political Rights (1966) upon the British government with respect to Northern Ireland. The reason why seems quite obvious to me: The British government has absolutely no defense under basic principles of international law for the gross and consistent pattern of fundamental human rights violations that it has historically perpetrated against the Catholic population of Northern Ireland. To his great credit, Mr. Carrick did not expend any time attempting to defend the indefensible.

6. Likewise with respect to paragraph 17, Mr. Carrick's reference to the European Convention on Human Rights is completely misleading. Up until the current point in time, the British parliament has always refused to enact domestic implementing legislation for the European Convention on Human Rights that would be required to effectuate its provisions as a matter of internal British law. This consistent refusal by the British government to enact the European Convention on Human Rights into domestic law means that Catholics living in Northern Ireland cannot plead a cause of action on the basis of the European Convention in a British court, thus effectively denying them the direct protections of the Convention. This longstanding policy of the British government has violated articles 1 and 13 of the European Convention on Human Rights:

> *Article 1.* The High Contracting Parties shall secure to everyone within their jurisdiction the rights and freedoms defined in Section I of this Convention.

> *Article 13.* Everyone whose rights and freedoms as set forth in this Convention are violated shall have an effective

remedy before a national authority notwithstanding that
the violation has been committed by persons acting in an
official capacity.

The reason why the British government has consistently opposed implementing legislation for the European Convention has been for the express purpose of making sure that Catholics in Northern Ireland—as well as Blacks and Asiatics living in Great Britain—will not have the opportunity to plead a cause of action under the European Convention in a British court. The hypocritical stance of the British government over its refusal to enact implementing legislation for the European Convention on Human Rights simply confirms the substance of my *Memorandum* and also provides additional compelling evidence of the need for the MacBride Principles.

7. Similarly in paragraph 17, Mr. Carrick objects to my reference to the Genocide Convention of 1948, which has recently received the advice and consent of the United States Senate. Perhaps Mr. Carrick should actually read the terms of the Convention itself. If so, he would discover that the Convention makes it quite clear that genocide can be committed in a number of ways other than simply by means of killing individuals. To quote from article 2 of the Genocide Convention:

In the present Convention, genocide means any of the
following acts committed with intent to destroy, in whole
or in part, a national, ethnical, racial or *religious* group
as such:
(a)   Killing members of the group;
(b)   *Causing serious bodily or mental harm to
      members of the group;*
(c)   *Deliberately inflicting on the group
      conditions of life calculated to bring about
      its physical destruction in whole or in part*
      . . . .

Likewise, article 3 of the Genocide Convention provides that complicity in genocide is an international crime in its own right. Genocide Convention article 4 provides that persons committing genocide or complicity in genocide shall be punished whether they are constitutionally responsible rulers, public officials or private individuals. Hence my conclusion that under the terms of the Genocide Convention, the State of Illinois would certainly have an obligation to investigate and determine whether or not its pension funds are being used for the purpose of committing genocide as defined by articles 2(b) and 2(c) in order to avoid creating any risk of accomplice liability under the terms of articles 3 and 4. Thus the need for H.B. 1374.

8. This obligation to investigate becomes irresistibly compelling in a situation where the British government knows full well that a disproportionately high degree of unemployment for Catholics has encouraged their emigration from Northern Ireland. Based upon two trips to Northern Ireland during the past year, I have found evidence tending to indicate that government officials there favor continuing disproportionately high unemployment for Catholics in order to encourage their emigration from Northern Ireland for the express purpose of maintaining a Protestant majority in that province for the indefinite future. A governmental policy of encouraging or tolerating high unemployment for Catholics in order to produce their emigration from Northern Ireland for such reasons would constitute grave breaches of articles 1, 2(b), 2(c), 3 and 4 of the Genocide Convention. I repeat: The State of Illinois must investigate this situation in order to determine whether or not its pension fund investments are being used to violate fundamental norms of international human rights law against Catholics in Northern Ireland.

9. In my *Memorandum* I have already discussed at great length the reasons why the MacBride Principles do not violate the terms of the Fair Employment Act. This was also the ruling of U.S. Federal District Judge Robert Carter in *New York City Employees' Retirement System vs. American Brands*, 634 F. Supp. 1382 (S.D.N.Y. 1986). Mr. Carrick is certainly correct to point out that ultimately this question can only be definitively answered by a British court. I submit that an unbiased and objective British court—two conditions that would disqualify all the courts in Northern Ireland on this question—would reach precisely the same conclusion as did Judge Carter. The British government is a party to the 1965 International Convention on the Elimination of All Forms of Racial Discrimination. Article I(4) of that Convention provides as follows:

> Special measures taken for the sole purpose of securing adequate advancement of certain racial or ethnic groups or individuals requiring such protection as may be necessary in order to ensure to such groups or individuals equal enjoyment or exercise of human rights and fundamental freedoms shall not be deemed racial discrimination, provided, however, that such measures do not, as a consequence, lead to the maintenance of separate rights for different racial groups and that they

shall not be continued after the objectives for which they were taken have been achieved.

To the extent that the MacBride Principles would require measures of affirmative action for Catholics in Northern Ireland, such measures would be fully consistent with article I(4) of the International Convention on the Elimination of All Forms of Racial Discrimination, to which the British government is a party. By signing this Convention, the British government has already taken the official position that affirmative action programs such as those called for in the MacBride Principles are not a form of racial discrimination or reverse discrimination against anyone. For this reason as well, therefore, the MacBride Principles would not violate the Fair Employment Act.

Conclusion

I believe this disposes of the main points in the Carrick Critique. I wish to conclude this letter, however, by repeating the following language taken from the Introduction to my *Memorandum*:

> In my professional judgment, the enactment of H.B. 1374 (or its successor) would constitute a positive step toward alleviation of the official and unofficial discrimination that is currently being practiced and tolerated on grounds of religion and political opinion in Northern Ireland against the Catholic population of that province. Furthermore, the enactment of this legislation by the Illinois General Assembly would be fully consistent with international law, United States law, and the laws of the State of Illinois. Finally, the passage of H.B. 1374 would generate some small but very positive momentum toward a peaceful resolution of the fundamental dispute over the ultimate status of Northern Ireland.

Nothing in the Carrick Critique or in the testimony of his associates before the House Committee on State and Government Administration on June 16 has altered these conclusions. Indeed, as explained above, in some respects the Carrick Critique has only strengthened these conclusions by adducing further compelling reasons in support of the MacBride Principles.

If there is any other way in which I can be of assistance to you or your colleagues in your deliberations on H.B. 1374, please feel free to get in touch with me directly. Thank you very much for your kind consideration in this matter. It has been most appreciated.

Yours very truly,

Francis A. Boyle
Professor of Law

encl's.

cc's.: Lieutenant Governor George Ryan
The Honorable Michael J. Madigan, Speaker, House of Representatives
The Honorable Philip J. Rock, President, Illinois Senate
Senator Judy Baar Topinka
Senator J. E. Joyce
Senator Richard F. Kelly, Jr.
The Honorable Lee A. Daniels, Minority Leader
The Honorable David Harris, Minority Spokesman
Representative John J. Cullerton
Representative Jack L. Kubik
Representative Roger P. McAuliffe
Representative James F. Keane
Representative Andrew J. McGann
All members of the Illinois House Committee on State Government Administration.

*　　　　*　　　　*　　　　*

Irish National Caucus, Inc.

NEWS RELEASE
CONTACT: FATHER SEAN McMANUS
Phone (202) 544-0568
Fax (202) 543-2491

Boycott Companies and Lobbyists
Working Against MacBride

Washington, DC, February 3, 1993. Law firms and lobbyists hired by the British Government or others to lobby against the MacBride Principles now face a Boycott by Irish Americans.

The Boycott was launched by the Irish National Caucus—the group that launched the MacBride Principles.

Speaking from the Caucus headquarters on Capitol Hill, Washington, DC, Father Seán McManus, President, said: "Companies that lobby against the MacBride Principles—whether on behalf of the British Government or others—should be boycotted by all Irish Americans concerned about anti-Catholic discrimination in Northern Ireland. What would African Americans and Jewish Americans do to companies that were profiting from racism or anti-Semitism? We Irish Americans must do like-wise. We must make it clear that there is a price to pay for supporting anti-Catholic discrimination in Northern Ireland."

Chicago Company and IBM First Targets

The first companies to be targeted are the Chicago law company Sidley & Austin and I.B.M.

"This arose," explained Father McManus, "out of a discussion I had with Professor Francis Boyle of the University of Illinois. who is a leader of the MacBride Bill campaign and the author of a MacBride Bill before the Chicago City Council."

Sidley & Austin has been hired by IBM to lobby against the MacBride Principles in the Chicago City Council. On October 1. 1992, Mary A. Dempsey, of Sidley & Austin, wrote to Alderman Patrick J. O'Connor: "Signing the [MacBride] Principles directly contravenes official United States State Department policy on this issue. As an American corporation also doing business in Northern Ireland. we feel compelled to comply with our government's policy."

"And we feel compelled to launch a Boycott against Sidley & Austin and IBM," stated Fr. McManus.

"We call on Irish Americans working in Sidley & Austin to quit their jobs. We call on those who have accounts with Sidley & Austin to withdraw those accounts. And we call on Irish Americans to Boycott Sidley & Austin branches in Los Angeles, New York, and Washington DC. And we call on people concerned with fairness and equality and who abhor discrimination to Boycott Sidley & Austin in London, Singapore and Tokyo. And we call for a complete Boycott of all I.B.M. products."

Pariah Firms

Francis Boyle. a professor of law, said: "What I.B.M. and Sidley & Austin have done in Chicago is reprehensible: promoting discrimination against Irish Catholics in Northern Ireland. All Irish Catholic lawyers, law students, Business-people and consumers must immediately terminate any business relationships they might have with these two pariah firms. Our People in Northern Ireland would demand nothing less from us."

The Irish National Caucus will add to the Boycott list other law and lobby firms that lobby against MacBride as they become known.

The Caucus has three effective Boycotts already going: Ford Motor Company, Timex Watches and Coca-Cola.

*   *   *   *

Endnotes

1   Omnibus Consolidated and Emergency Appropriations Act, Pub. L. 105-277, 112 Stat. 2681 § 2811 (1998). *See generally* Kevin McNamara, The MacBride Principles (Liverpool Univ. Press: 2009)

2   British Consul General in Chicago.

CHAPTER SEVEN

SPARING
ROBERT JOHN MACBRIDE

Sean MacBride's father, John, was a hero and martyr of the 1916 Easter Rebellion. But before that, John had fought Britain in the Second Boer War (1899-1902) when he helped organize and command the Irish Transvaal Brigade consisting of about 500 Irish and Irish Americans on behalf of the Boer Republic. John was commissioned a Major by the Boer government.

While in South Africa, John sired offspring leading, generations later, to the birth of his great-grandson, Robert John MacBride, who is of mixed-race. In the spirit of his great-grandfather before him, Robert joined the ranks of the armed wing of Nelson Mandela's African National Congress (A.N.C.) as a soldier in order to fight against the Boers and their criminal apartheid regime. Pursuant to their instructions, he attacked a so-called "soft target" in which civilians were killed. Robert MacBride was sentenced to death with the execution to take place in the immediate future and at any time without prior notice.

Immediately upon reading of Robert's plight, I resolved: This shall not stand! There was no way I was going to let the Boers kill the great-grandson of Major John MacBride!

At that time, I was on the Board of Directors of Amnesty International USA (1988-1992). So I immediately called up our Executive Director Jack Healey—my friend, fellow Irish American, and a long-time friend of Sean MacBride. Jack readily agreed that he would assume personal responsibility for mobilizing a worldwide campaign by Amnesty International to prevent the execution of Robert John MacBride. Amnesty International is an abolitionist organization that vigorously opposes the execution of any human being for any reason. Sean was one of Amnesty's founders. I knew Jack would take this mission personally.

Then I turned to implement the second element of my plan to spare Robert John MacBride from execution. Previously, Sean had told me that the Boer government in South Africa considered his father to be a great national hero and indeed had erected a Memorial to him and the Irish Brigade who had fought on the side of the Boer Republic against Britain in their capital Pretoria. Therefore, whenever Sean visited South Africa, he would always make it a point to ask the Boer government to spare the life of one A.N.C. soldier sentenced to death. Out of respect for Sean's father Major John (not Sean), the Boer government would always do so.

By this time Sean was dead. But I figured I would carry out this task for him to spare Robert John MacBride. I would personally call in the debt that the Boers owed to Major John MacBride.

So after speaking with Jack Healey, I then immediately called up the Consul General of South Africa in Chicago and had a lengthy conversation with him about this matter. I asked him in the name of Major John MacBride and the MacBride Family to convey a request by me to the President of South Africa to issue a reprieve for the life of Robert John MacBride. To his everlasting credit, the Consul General of South Africa agreed to convey my request to their President. Here is what I had to say to the Consul General and their President:

*   *   *   *

December 28, 1988

The Honorable Daniel Smith
Consul-General of South Africa
Consulate of South Africa
200 South Michigan Avenue
Chicago, Illinois 60604

Dear Mr. Smith:

Just a short note to follow up on the conversation we had last week over the telephone. I am writing to request that the South African government give serious consideration to sparing the life of Robert John MacBride. I realize of course that he has been sentenced to death for committing offenses of a most serious nature under South African law. However, the fate of Mr. MacBride is of enormous concern to his fellow Irishmen and Irishwomen here in the United States.

Robert John MacBride is the great-grandson of Major John MacBride, who was martyred by the British government for the part he played in the 1916 Easter Rebellion in Dublin, Ireland. Prior to those momentous events that ultimately resulted in the liberation of the Irish people from the awesome yoke of British colonial imperialism, John MacBride had left Ireland in 1895 to work as a journalist in South Africa. When the Boer War broke out, John MacBride courageously and unselfishly led a party of 300 Irish volunteers fighting against the British on behalf of the Boers. When the Boer uprising was finally crushed with harsh brutality by the British, Major MacBride had to depart South Africa. Nevertheless, as I understand it, John MacBride is still honored as a great hero in the Republic of South Africa and his Irish volunteers are still remembered with a great deal of respect and admiration by the South African people.

Eventually, John MacBride was executed by the British, which was the same enemy he had voluntarily fought on behalf of the Boers. It would constitute a most unfortunate set of tragic circumstances if his great-grandson, Robert John MacBride, were now to be executed by the successor to the Boer Republic. The MacBride Family has already paid an incredible price for their valiant struggle against British colonial imperialism, whether in Ireland or South Africa.

As an Irish American, it is therefore my personal hope that your State President will graciously decide to exercise clemency in the case of Robert John MacBride in order to spare the MacBride Family from suffering yet another personal tragedy. I would respectfully submit that President Botha now has an opportunity to pay back the debt owed by the Boers to John MacBride and the Irish volunteers by sparing the life of his great-grandson. I can assure you that if this were to occur, the Government of South Africa would earn the gratitude of the Irish American community here in the United States.

I do hope you will have the opportunity to convey my viewpoints on this matter directly to your government in Pretoria. I want to thank you very much for your kind consideration in this matter. It has been most appreciated.

Yours very truly,

Francis A. Boyle
Professor of Law

The Boers never killed Robert John MacBride. An attempt was made to assassinate him on the way out of prison, but he recovered from his wounds. The last I read Robert was a Police Captain in the apartheid-free Republic of South Africa.

I have never met or even communicated with Robert John MacBride. But it was a great honor and distinct privilege for me to have had a role to play in sparing the great-grandson of Ireland's great national hero Major John MacBride. We Irish owe him so much. It was the least I could do for him:

....

> This other man I had dreamed
> A drunken, vainglorious lout.
> He had done most bitter wrong
> To some who are near my heart,
> Yet I number him in the song;
> He, too, has resigned his part
> In the casual comedy;
> He, too, has been changed in his turn,
> Transformed utterly:
> A terrible beauty is born.
> ...
> I write it out in a verse—
> MacDonagh and MacBride
> And Connolly and Pearse
> Now and in time to be,
> Wherever green is worn,
> Are changed, changed utterly:
> A terrible beauty is born.

The Force runs strong in the MacBride family: Major John MacBride, his wife Maude Gonne, their son Sean, John's great-grandson Robert John. Three generations of Irish Revolutionaries having fought in three different revolutionary wars on two different continents during the course of the twentieth century. Wherever you find the Poor, the Oppressed, and the Downtrodden of the World fighting against injustice, and tyranny, and violence, and persecution, there you will find Irish helping them out.

CHAPTER EIGHT

DESIGNING
UNITED IRELAND

      This chapter is intended to provide some preliminary suggestions for the design of United Ireland from the perspective of international law and human rights. Obviously it is not intended to deal with all the weighty complications that would surround the establishment of United Ireland. These could only be decided by all of the people living on the entire Island of Ireland—the one and only self-determination unit for Ireland—exercising their right of self-determination under international law and human rights. Rather, I intend to generate some ideas for all Irish people now to consider, discuss, debate, criticize, reject, and improve upon concerning how to establish what I am here, for convenience, calling United Ireland, in the not-too-distant future. It is offered as an impressionistic first-cut at United Ireland.

Creating a New State

      Let me start with the preliminary observation that United Ireland should not be established by having the current Republic of Ireland consisting of only 26 counties simply gobble up and incorporate the remaining 6 counties that are currently called Northern Ireland together with its inhabitants. I respectfully submit that Protestants living in Northern Ireland would vigorously and rightfully object to being engulfed by and annexed into the State currently known as the Republic of Ireland. Rather, we all need to start with a tabula rasa, a blank slate.

      This can be done by all the people currently living on the Island of Ireland deciding to set up a completely new State that I will hereinafter call United Ireland (U.I.) consisting of all 32 counties in order to distinguish it from the currently existing twenty-six county Republic of Ireland (R.O.I). **Let all the people living on the Island of Ireland come together and design and create a completely new State!** This United Ireland would be the Successor State in Law to as well as the Legal Continuator of (1) the Republic of Ireland; (2) the 1916 Irish Republic; and (3) the 6 counties on the Island of Ireland known today as Northern Ireland.

      In this manner United Ireland would carry on all three different legal entities and political traditions on the Island of Ireland today. Not one of these three legal entities and political traditions would be extinguished, but rather all three would be merged into and continued by the new State of United Ireland. Thus, by means of establishing United Ireland in this way, proper consideration and respect would be afforded to Protestants and to the Protestant tradition in Northern Ireland.

Naming the New State

      I doubt very seriously that Protestants would want to live in a state called the Republic of Ireland, let alone the Irish Republic. The precise name of the new state does not really matter because it can always be given a republican system of government by means of its constitution without officially denominating the new state as a Republic. For example, the United States of America is a Republic without officially calling itself by that name.

      Here I have suggested United Ireland along the lines of the United Kingdom: United Ireland resulting from the union of the Republic of Ireland and Northern Ireland replacing United Kingdom consisting of Great Britain and its colonial appendage, Northern Ireland. United Ireland for short. At the end of the day the Irish People will have to decide for themselves what to name their new state by means of a referendum. At that time, perhaps the best that could be agreed upon is simply to call their new state both Ireland and Eire—since it will be officially bilingual. I have chosen to use United Ireland in this book as a symbolic place-holder pending that day.

State Succession

      As the Successor in Law to and the Legal Continuator of the Republic of Ireland, United Ireland would take R.O.I's place as the contracting party to all international treaties, agreements, and assurances currently concluded in the name of the Republic of Ireland. This State Succession and Continuation would include R.O.I's membership in all international organizations and especially in the entirety of the United Nations System and the European Union System. Hence there would be no legal discontinuity whatsoever when it comes to the international legal personality and democratic representation for all the people living on the Island of Ireland. But it would be more than just a change of names from Republic of Ireland to United Ireland. United Ireland would be a completely new State under international law and practice that would be designed and created by all the people living on the Island of Ireland exercising together their fundamental right to self-determination.

Human Rights

Thus, United Ireland would also automatically succeed the Republic of Ireland as a contracting party to all the human rights treaties to which the Republic of Ireland is currently a contracting party, including and especially the European Convention on Human Rights. Furthermore, since all people living in Northern Ireland today are entitled to the benefits of all the human rights treaties to which the United Kingdom (U.K.) is currently a contracting party, United Ireland must become a contracting party to all U.K. human rights treaties that the Republic of Ireland is not currently a contracting party to. This is because the human rights guaranteed by these U.K. human rights treaties have already been vested in the people currently living in Northern Ireland. They cannot and must not be deprived of these, their basic human rights.

In this manner the Protestants currently living in Northern Ireland would continue to benefit from all human rights treaties to which the United Kingdom is currently a contracting party. In addition, all the people currently living in the Republic of Ireland would also benefit by United Ireland becoming a contracting party to U.K. human rights treaties to which the Republic of Ireland is not a contracting party. Furthermore, then all of these human rights treaties must be specifically enacted into domestic law by the Parliament of United Ireland so that any person living on the Island of Ireland could go into court and get his or her basic human rights enforced directly under any one or more of these treaties.[1] In this manner, United Ireland would be a "win-win" solution for all the people living on the Island of Ireland when it comes to protecting and promoting their basic human rights.

Religion

One of the most fundamental human rights of all is the right to freedom of religion. Article 18 of the Universal Declaration of Human Rights (1948) has specified this basic human right by means of the following language: "Everyone has the right to freedom of thought, conscience and religion; this right includes freedom to change his religion or belief, and freedom, either alone or in community with others and in public or private, to manifest his religion or belief in teaching, practice, worship and observance." The Constitution for United Ireland should expressly incorporate *in haec verba* the entirety of the Universal Declaration of Human Rights, and provide that the U.D.H.R. is self-executing as a matter of domestic law enforcement by all judges and government officials. The U.D.H.R. should become the Bill of Rights for the United Ireland Constitution along the lines of the first Ten Amendments to the United States Constitution—America's Bill of Rights.

It is undeniable that the Republic of Ireland historically has been and currently still is a confessional state in favor of Catholicism. Therefore extra protections must be taken to guarantee that Protestants living in United Ireland will be able to believe and worship and practice their religion as they see fit. In other words, United Ireland must not be a confessional state.

To accomplish this objective, I respectfully recommend that the Constitution of United Ireland expressly incorporate the two Religion Clauses of the First Amendment to the United States Constitution: "Congress shall make no law respecting an establishment of religion, or prohibiting the free exercise thereof..." The (non)-Establishment Clause and the Free Exercise Clause of the First Amendment to the United States Constitution have done an excellent job of preserving and protecting and promoting a multitude of religions, and religious beliefs, and religious practices, in an American Society that identifies itself as predominantly Christian. These two Religion Clauses drawn from the First Amendment to the United States Constitution could likewise serve to preserve, protect, defend, and promote Protestant beliefs and practices as well the Protestant tradition in United Ireland.

Finally, out of an excess of caution, I would also recommend that the United Ireland Constitution incorporate the following language taken from Article VI, Clause 3 of the United States Constitution: "...no religious Test shall ever be required as a Qualification to any Office or public Trust under the United States." These three Religion Clauses of the United States Constitution have done an outstanding job at promoting religious diversity in the United States of America. I submit the same can be done for United Ireland with its long-standing Protestant, Catholic, and Jewish religious traditions and heritages. The same principle would also hold true for the other religious minorities in United Ireland as well as for secularists.

Language

In the preceding section I argued that we must bend over

backwards to protect the religious rights of Protestants living in United Ireland. By the same token, we also need to guarantee the basic human right of people to speak the Irish language in United Ireland. This is because of the long and sordid effort by Britain to extirpate the Irish language. Therefore, the Constitution for United Ireland should make the State officially bilingual: Irish and English. It could be similar to the constitutional arrangement in Canada where both English and French are the official languages. The practical details would have to be worked out and implemented by the Parliament of United Ireland.

Property

Most of the land in Northern Ireland was stolen by Britain from the indigenous Irish inhabitants. Therefore Protestants living today in Northern Ireland might fear for good cause that their real property and their personal property could be at legal risk in United Ireland. Therefore in order to calm their fears, I would respectfully recommend that the Constitution for United Ireland incorporate language taken directly from the Fifth Amendment to the United States Constitution along the following lines: "No person shall be...deprived of life, liberty, or property, without due process of law; nor shall private property be taken for public use without just compensation." This language should be sufficient to copper-fasten their interests in real property and in personal property for Protestants living in United Ireland.

Citizenship, Nationality, and Residence

Another protection that could be afforded to Protestants in Northern Ireland would be for them to be able to retain their British citizenship while living in United Ireland. They would also retain their British passports and could have the British Parliament guarantee as a matter of domestic law their right (and that of their descendants) to reside in Britain forever. The British Parliament should also extend the same rights to Catholics and their descendants living in Northern Ireland on grounds of non-discrimination. Moreover, the British Parliament could enact legislation to permit British citizens living in United Ireland to vote in British elections by means of an absentee ballot as well as to be elected to public office in Britain.

Protestants (and Catholics) living in Northern Ireland should also be entitled to claim citizenship in United Ireland and thus become dual nationals if they so desire. On the other hand, Northern Ireland Protestants and their descendants (as well as Catholics and their descendants) should not be forced to accept Irish citizenship or nationality in United Ireland if they do not want to. Nevertheless, such individuals (and their descendants) should still retain their right of permanent residence in United Ireland.

To be sure, if such individuals choose to remain living in United Ireland as exclusively British citizens, then they would be bound to obey the laws of United Ireland—just as is true for permanent residents living in any other country. Nevertheless, they would still be entitled to invoke all the protections of the international and domestic human rights regime outlined above. Moreover, since they are currently residents on the Island of Ireland, such individuals should have the basic right to participate in the drafting of a new Constitution for United Ireland that would contain within itself a Bill of Rights protecting all the people who live in Ireland irrespective of citizenship and nationality, let alone religion and language.

Furthermore, under that new Constitution, such individuals should be permitted to vote in whatever type of Irish elections they so desire on the basis of their qualifications as permanent residents in United Ireland. In this way, communities living in today's Northern Ireland that consist of a majority of Protestants could continue to maintain majority political control over local, municipal, and county-wide governmental bodies in United Ireland, subject to the non-discrimination regime mentioned above. Indeed, this new Irish Constitution should accord such permanent residents of United Ireland all of the legal, political, and constitutional rights of Irish citizens without any distinction. These rights should include those of full and equal participation in voting, law-making, governance, administration, adjudication, public office-holding, education, etc. Of course such individuals would remain free to exercise or not exercise any one or more of these fundamental rights guaranteed to them by the new Constitution. But for all functional purposes, there should be no constitutional or legal or human rights distinctions whatsoever drawn between these Protestant (and Catholic) permanent residents and citizens in United Ireland.

No point would be served here by continuing to spell out the multifarious constitutional, legal, political, and human rights protections that could be designed for Protestants—with their active participation—who would be living in United Ireland. Suffice it to say that enormous progress can be made in this direction by breaking down and distinguishing the rights pertaining to (1) citizenship; (2) nationality; (3) residence; (4) voting; and (5) governance in United Ireland. Fortunately, all these questions will be made incredibly easy to handle and therefore quite flexible to negotiate because both Britain and Ireland are today members of the European Union (E.U.) and thus bound by the various protections and privileges afforded to citizens of E.U. member states without discrimination·

A Template for United Ireland's Constitution

Obviously this is neither the time nor the place to draft a Constitution for United Ireland that would cover all the basic details necessary to establish this new state. But I would like to suggest a model constitution for all the Irish people to consider in drafting United Ireland's Constitution. Britain does not have a written constitution. Protestants would rightly object to modeling the United Ireland Constitution on the Constitution for the Republic of Ireland.

Therefore, with all due respect and humility, as a compromise alternative, I would like to suggest that the Irish consider the Constitution for the United States of America as Amended— with all its defects and faults—as a template to be used for drafting the United Ireland Constitution. In 1787 the U.S Constitution emerged out of a Protestant political culture, heritage, and philosophy. Since then, comparatively speaking, the U.S Constitution has done a pretty good job of promoting a multiethnic, multi-religious, multiracial republic. It can do the same for United Ireland.

Truth and Reconciliation

In post-Good Friday Northern Ireland there has been some talk about establishing a Truth and Reconciliation Process. I respectfully submit that these intimations are, and such discussions would be, premature. How could there possibly be any degree of "truth," let alone "reconciliation," while Britain continues to occupy even one square millimeter of Ireland? The institution of a Truth and Reconciliation process at this time would simply constitute a white-wash, a cover-up, and an immunization of the long history of British crimes against the Irish in Northern Ireland, in the Republic of Ireland, and even in Britain itself. For this reason, a Truth and Reconciliation process at this time would only significantly delay Britain's departure from Ireland. Why would we Irish want to do that prior to the British departure from Ireland?

That being said, the establishment of a Truth and Reconciliation process should be an integral component for the foundation of United Ireland. The Constitution for United Ireland could call for the creation of a Truth and Reconciliation Commission. Thereunder, any person could appear before the Commission and admit to conduct involving acts of violence against persons and property in Ireland and Britain that had a political motivation behind them, and then answer any questions the members of the Commission might have about them. The Commission would then be authorized and directed to grant full-scale political and legal immunity—both criminal and civil—for all the conduct admitted before it. This immunity would be constitutionally valid and binding and obligatory for all legal and political purposes throughout United Ireland.

In addition, the British Parliament would also have to adopt domestic legislation granting both political as well as civil and criminal legal immunity for any conduct admitted to before United Ireland's Truth and Reconciliation Commission for which the latter has granted immunity. Thus, even British citizens living in Britain could appear before the United Ireland Truth and Reconciliation Commission, admit their activity, and receive full political and legal immunity that would be effective in both United Ireland and Britain. With the establishment of United Ireland it would be critical, and indeed possible, to promote Truth and Reconciliation between Protestants and Catholics living in United Ireland, as well as Truth and Reconciliation between the Irish People and the British People, as well as Truth and Reconciliation between United Ireland and Britain.

State Responsibility

Of course the above-described Truth and Reconciliation process would only deal with personal legal responsibility for individual human beings still living. It would not affect the obligation by Britain to pay reparations for genocide to United Ireland for the Irish Hecatomb as detailed in chapter 1 and for the other atrocities that Britain has inflicted upon Ireland and the Irish over the centuries. This is a matter of State Responsibility incumbent upon Britain under international law. Satisfaction of this issue of State Responsibility will still have to be established by means of negotiation, arbitration, adjudication, etc. between Britain and United Ireland as required by articles 2 (3) and 33 of the United Nations Charter.

Conclusion

In this manner, with the establishment of United Ireland both Protestants and Catholics living on the Island of Ireland as well as the Irish People and the British People should be able to draw a line beneath the past nine centuries of struggle and strife and genocide in order to move forward from there as equals. But this cannot possibly happen until Britain finally leaves Ireland *in toto*. Furthermore, when Britain finally leaves its very first colony in Ireland, and if the British People reconcile with the Irish People as indicated above, then perhaps it might be possible for Britain to reconcile with its other genocidal and colonial victims around the world in a similar manner.

In any event, the proverbial handwriting is on the wall for the illegal colonial settler enclave known today as Northern Ireland for all the world to see but the willfully blind. United Ireland is an historic inevitability. If not tomorrow, then certainly within a generation. We Irish must make the prospect of United Ireland as attractive and non-threatening as possible to our Protestant brothers and sisters living in Northern Ireland while at the same time remaining true to our Republican values and principles.

Endnotes

1   *See generally* Irish Human Rights Commission, Submission for the Twelfth Session of the Working Group on the Universal Periodic Review: Ireland (March 2011).

INDEX